# NANCY REAGAN

## A First Lady's Style

# NANCY REAGAN

## A First Lady's Style

Ronald Reagan Presidential Library Foundation

This book is published in conjunction with the
exhibition *Nancy Reagan—A First Lady's Style*
The Ronald Reagan Presidential Library and Museum
Simi Valley, California
November 10, 2007 through November 10, 2008

Published and organized by The Ronald Reagan
Presidential Library Foundation
Frederick J. Ryan, Jr., Chairman of the Board of Trustees

Exhibition and catalogue produced by
WRJ Design Associates, LLC
Rush Jenkins, Principal
Kate Holt, Project Manager

Essays by Bob Colacello and Kirby Hanson
Contributions by Adolfo, Diane von Furstenberg,
James Galanos, Valentino Garavani, Carolina Herrera,
and Oscar de la Renta

Edited by Elisa Urbanelli
Designed by Miko McGinty and Doug Clouse
Photography of clothing by Stefan Studer
Color separations by Professional Graphics,
    Rockford, Illinois
Printed by CS Graphics, Singapore

Library of Congress Control Number: 2007933931

ISBN 978-0-9798300-0-6

Published by
The Ronald Reagan Presidential Library Foundation
40 Presidential Drive
Simi Valley, California 93065

PHOTOGRAPHY CREDITS:

Cover and page 12: © The White House Historical
Association

Pages 3, 4, 5, 6, 7, 24: © 1978 John Engstead / MPTV.net

Pages 8, 56: © AP Images

Pages 16, 44, 49, 57 (top), 68, 94, 98, 99, 116, 142, 152
(right), 159, 162, 210, 211, 215 (bottom), 220: By Michael
Evans, courtesy of the Ronald Reagan Presidential Library

Pages 23, 26, 27, 29, 30, 32, 33, 34 (left), 51, 55 (middle
and right), 61 (right), 109 (left), 171 (bottom right):
Courtesy of the Nancy Reagan Private Photo Collection

Page 37: © 1978 Wallace Seawell / MPTV.net

Page 39: Courtesy of the Richard Nixon Presidential
Library

Page 41: © Bettmann/CORBIS

Page 45: By Horst P. Horst. Courtesy of the Condé Nast
Archive

Page 228: © Dirck Halstead from the Dirck Halstead
collection, Center for American History

Pages 242, 243, 244, 245: Courtesy of Pete Souza/
Ronald Reagan Presidential Library Foundation

All mannequin and detail photos by Stefan Studer, courtesy
of the Ronald Reagan Presidential Library

All other photos from the White House Photo Collection,
courtesy of the Ronald Reagan Presidential Library

ON THE COVER : Portrait of Nancy Reagan by Aaron
Shikler, courtesy of the White House Historical Association.

PAGES 2–3: Nancy Reagan (née Davis) in Hollywood
publicity photos from 1949–1951.

PAGE 4: Nancy Reagan in the doorway of her home,
General Electric's "House of the Future," on San Onofre
Drive in Pacific Palisades.

PAGS 5: The governor and first lady of California in a
1960s portrait.

PAGE 6: Nancy Reagan at the Malibu ranch, "Yearling
Row," in the 1960s.

PAGE 7: The Reagans at their Malibu ranch.

PAGE 8: President and Mrs. Reagan cross the South Lawn
of the White House.

# CONTENTS

# FOREWORD

The Ronald Reagan Presidential Library Foundation is proud to present the exhibition *Nancy Reagan—A First Lady's Style*. Beginning with her marriage to Ronald Reagan in 1952, through her years as California's first lady, and then as our country's first lady, this historic exhibition documents and celebrates the style of Nancy Reagan.

From the moment the Reagans first moved into the White House, they represented hope for America. Ronald Reagan's optimism, coupled with his wife's classic elegance, brought new inspiration to Washington. Attempting to capture the excitement, this exhibition looks back to the memorable period in our country's history when Ronald and Nancy Reagan occupied the White House, or "your house which you're letting us live in for a while," as the President remarked.

Nancy Reagan respected the historic significance of her role as America's first lady. Taking her responsibility seriously, she represented the country with grace and dignity, whether entertaining heads of state in the White House, promoting her "Just Say No" anti-drug campaign, or working with the Foster Grandparents program. By her husband's side, she was his treasured partner and lifelong love.

The exhibition and this publication provide an exceptional glimpse into the life and times of Nancy Reagan, as well as her influence, which continues today. We are deeply grateful to Mrs. Reagan for her significant contribution to the exhibition and her dedication to the Ronald Reagan Presidential Library in Simi Valley, California.

On behalf of the Board of Directors of the Ronald Reagan Presidential Library Foundation, we hope you enjoy *Nancy Reagan—A First Lady's Style*.

FREDERICK J. RYAN, JR.
*Chairman, Ronald Reagan Presidential Library Foundation*

The official White House portrait of Nancy Reagan, painted by Aaron Shikler and presented to the White House Historical Association on January 17, 1989, currently hangs in the White House.

# PREFACE

It has been a pleasure and tremendous honor to undertake the design of the Ronald Reagan Presidential Library Foundation's exhibition *Nancy Reagan— A First Lady's Style*. This exhibition and catalogue are a celebration of Nancy Reagan's inimitable style and her tenure as first lady of the United States.

Some eighty dresses and suits worn by Mrs. Reagan are highlighted in the galleries of the Library, all chosen for their historic significance, exquisite workmanship, and embodiment of Mrs. Reagan's signature style. The exhibition spans more than thirty years, commencing with the wedding suit Nancy Davis wore on March 4, 1952, when she and Ronald Reagan exchanged their wedding vows at the Little Brown Church in the valley. Ensembles worn during Mrs. Reagan's term as the first lady of California and the presidential campaign of 1980 build up to the primary focus of the exhibition—Mrs. Reagan's style as our country's first lady. The exhibition concludes with the suit designed by James Galanos that she wore when President Reagan's casket was brought to the Capitol for the state funeral in 2004.

Mrs. Reagan enthusiastically embraced her mission of returning the White House to an international symbol of beauty, elegance, and dignity befitting America's grandest home. Carolina Herrera once wrote, "It's difficult to define style. It's not what you are wearing but how you wear it. It's a personal thing and reflected in the way you arrange your house, your taste in books and art—the personal stamp you give to everything you touch." It can be said that Mrs. Reagan's style was quintessentially American—classic and effortless—and everything from how she entertained to how she dressed as first lady bore the mark of her discerning eye for detail and understatement. Relying on some of the greatest fashion talents of the day, Mrs. Reagan turned to the sophisticated and beautifully made designs of Adolfo, Geoffrey Beene, Bill Blass, Chanel, James Galanos, Carolina Herrera, Oscar de la Renta, Valentino, and Yves Saint Laurent for her wardrobe.

The exhibition and its catalogue highlight many of the roles assumed by Mrs. Reagan as first lady, including hostess and ambassador, public servant and spokeswoman, and, most importantly, spouse of the president. She chose her wardrobe carefully for the numerous events she attended, always mindful that she represented our country. Whether attending state dinners in glamorous gowns by

Nancy Reagan in the Red Room of the White House.

Galanos and Valentino or visiting schools and clinics to promote the "Just Say No" and Foster Grandparents programs in a tailored Bill Blass dress or Oscar de la Renta suit, Mrs. Reagan displayed a style that was timeless.

Architectural elements extrapolated from the White House form the backdrop for the costumes on display, with photo montages and videos interwoven throughout the exhibition to help tell the story of Mrs. Reagan's roles, including the highs and lows every president and first lady experience while serving our country. This exhibition and catalogue are more than a show of designer dresses; they also tell the story of the love and partnership between a first lady and a president. The phrase "Behind every great man is a great woman" was never truer than with the Reagans.

On behalf of WRJ Design Associates, it has been a privilege to produce this exhibition and catalogue in honor of Mrs. Reagan and I hope that you enjoy this opportunity to share in the beauty of "a first lady's style."

RUSH JENKINS
*Principal, WRJ Design Associates*

An official White House portrait of Nancy Reagan in the Red Room.

# INTRODUCTION

## A LADY OF STYLE AND GRACE

### BOB COLACELLO

Whether in white sequins and diamonds for a state dinner, black suit and pearls for an audience with the pope, red sweater and slacks to decorate the White House Christmas tree with young people from a drug-treatment program, or gingham shirt and jeans for a horseback ride with the president at Rancho del Cielo, Nancy Reagan always looked just right. First lady of the United States is a job with many roles—and as the daughter of an actress who had been an actress herself, Mrs. Reagan was accustomed to quick costume changes. Whether performing as official White House hostess, representative of the nation on trips abroad, or promoter of such worthy causes as Foster Grandparents and "Just Say No," she displayed an acute sense of appropriateness in dress and manners, adhering to a firm belief that looking good and behaving correctly were obligations that went with her position. This was not as easy as it might seem, especially in a modern democratic republic, where the wives of political leaders are expected to be neither too grand nor too common—and an omnipresent media has little inhibition about pointing out excesses and deficiencies. As first lady, Nancy Reagan walked a fine line between refinement and naturalness, dignity and glamour. With the help of several outstanding American designers, including James Galanos, Bill Blass, Oscar de la Renta, Carolina Herrera, and Geoffrey Beene, and a few Europeans, notably Yves Saint Laurent, Valentino, and Karl Lagerfeld of Chanel, she achieved a look that was classic without being dowdy, fashionable but not trendy. It was a balancing act that required discipline, self-assurance, and an understanding of the subtle ways in which style can convey values and ideals.

She carried this aesthetic approach, or devotion to form, if you will, beyond her personal appearance to her surroundings, the veritable sets in which the story of a presidency is played out. In record-breaking time, she redecorated the White House from top to bottom, restoring the State Rooms to the polish and glory of the Kennedy years, and bringing a graciously comfortable California style to the private quarters with a mixture of antiques retrieved from a government warehouse and favorite pieces from the Reagans' house in Pacific Palisades. She spruced up the Oval Office to reflect Ronald Reagan's warm personality and set up a study at one end of the wide center hall that runs the length of the second floor where he could answer letters and

President and Mrs. Reagan pose on the Colonnade of the White House for
their thirty-fifth wedding anniversary portrait on March 3, 1987.

work on his speeches after office hours. In all of this she was greatly helped by the Los Angeles decorator Ted Graber, as well as longtime California friends who contributed or raised some $800,000, a large portion of which went to updating the old house's electrical wiring, plumbing, heating, and air-conditioning. She ordered new china, too, because, due to breakage over the years, the White House lacked a complete set of any one pattern, and she found a private foundation to cover the cost, a detail most of the press chose to ignore. Meanwhile, her close friend, Lenore Annenberg, who had been appointed chief of protocol, put the well-known New York decorators Mark Hampton and Mario Buatta to work on Blair House, the official government residence for visiting dignitaries, a project that was also privately funded.

The Reagans gave their first state dinner on February 26, 1981, barely a month after they moved into the White House. It was in honor of our closest ally, British Prime Minister Margaret Thatcher, and the guest list put together by Mrs. Reagan represented a savvy sampling of the best of America, from Old Hollywood stars Bob Hope and Charlton Heston to sculptor Louise Nevelson and Dance Theatre of Harlem director Arthur Mitchell, from New York philanthropist Brooke Astor and CBS founder William Paley to Kennedy Center chairman Roger Stevens and Washington *grande dame* Evangeline Bruce. White House chief usher Rex Scouten said that Mrs. Reagan took an intense interest in every detail, including the food, flowers, table settings, seating, and entertainment. Or as Muffie Brandon, the White House social secretary from 1981 to 1984, put it, in describing that first dinner, "Oh, the anemones on the green moiré tablecloths! It was magical! There was a sense of a new beginning—which was the slogan of the Reagan campaign. There was a sense of promise, and it was wonderful."

Before the end of that year, Nancy Reagan had overseen eight more state dinners, including back-to-back dinners in May—for Prime Minister Suzuki of Japan and Chancellor Schmidt of West Germany—the month after President Reagan was released from the hospital following the nearly successful attempt on his life. She also gave the first of many small private dinners in the upstairs Dining Room that month, in honor of Prince Charles, with another impressive guest list, including Mr. and Mrs. Paul Mellon, Mr. and Mrs. William F. Buckley, Diana Vreeland, Audrey Hepburn, Cary Grant, and Bobby Short, who tapped out some tunes on the piano after dessert. There were also dinners for King Juan Carlos of Spain, King Hussein of Jordan, President Sadat of Egypt, President Mitterrand of France, President Herrera of Venezuela, and Prime Minister Fraser of Australia in 1981. All told, President and Mrs. Reagan hosted fifty-seven state dinners during their eight years in the White House, far more than most of their predecessors. "The Reagans had such ease as hosts," recalled Muffie Brandon. "Mrs. Reagan always said to me, 'Muffie, these parties have to be fun.'"

"I loved giving state dinners," Mrs. Reagan has said. "When you think about it, they were easy: you had that great White House staff and that beautiful setting. And you could get a lot accomplished at state dinners, in terms of getting to know people and exchanging ideas." She asked the best performers America had to offer to entertain after dinner, whether they be opera singers like Leontyne Price and Frederica von Stade, jazz legends like Dave Brubeck and Ella Fitzgerald, classical musicians like Itzak Perlman and Van Cliburn, a modern dancer like Twyla Tharp, or a plain old crooner like Frank Sinatra. Every so often, she would throw in a foreign star like the Spanish singer Julio Iglesias or the exiled Russian cellist Mstislav Rostropovich. Social life in the Reagan White House was elegant and relaxed, international and bipartisan, with almost every guest list including prominent Democrats as well as Republicans. Like the first great White House hostess, Dolley Madison, Mrs. Reagan believed in "building bridges rather than bunkers" (to borrow a phrase from Madison's biographer, Catherine Allgor).

As important as state dinners were to her husband's diplomatic and political efforts, they were but a small part of Mrs. Reagan's duties as White House hostess. Her daily schedule was filled with an endless round of luncheons, cocktail receptions, press events, concerts, and screenings, each requiring an appropriate, fresh, and photogenic outfit. Her solution: Adolfo's versatile, stylish, figure-flattering, and wrinkle-free boucle knit suits, which could be worn all day long and into the evening. They also came in handy for the frequent trips Mrs. Reagan took on her own, most of them for her two primary causes: Foster Grandparents, which put lonely senior citizens together with needy adolescents and which she had become involved with as first lady of California; and the "Just Say No" anti-drug abuse program, which she launched in 1982. By 1989, she had logged more than 250,000 miles and visited hundreds of cities for "Just Say No" alone, touring rehabilitation centers, speaking at youth rallies, and talking with elementary and secondary schoolchildren about the dangers of addiction. On many other trips, Mrs. Reagan acted as a kind of ambassador without a portfolio, filling in for the president at important ceremonial events that he could not attend, such as the wedding of the Prince and Princess of Wales and the funeral of Princess Grace of Monaco. These occasions, of course, required more than a suitcase of Adolfos.

Although Nancy Reagan has said that her husband's decision to run for governor of California in 1966 "put us on a road we never intended to be on," everything in her background—a mix of society, showbiz, and medicine, with a touch of politics—seems to have prepared her for a life of high position. As her close friend Jerry Zipkin once said, "Nancy was reared up, not dragged up. It comes naturally to her to behave beautifully." Her adopted father, Dr. Loyal Davis, a prominent Chicago neurosurgeon, was a stickler for proper behavior and perfect grooming, and little Nancy did everything she could to please him. "My goodness, that man was very, very meticulous about his appearance and clothes," recalled family friend Abra Rockefeller Wilkin. Another old friend, Marjorie Everett, said, "I'm certain that some of the qualities we see in Nancy—the discipline especially—came from him." Her mother, the irrepressible and chic Edith Davis, was a tireless fundraiser for an array of charities, and totally dedicated to her husband's well-being. The famous friends she had met in her theater days, including Spencer Tracy, Katharine Hepburn, Walter Huston, and Lillian Gish, frequently stayed at the Davis apartment when they were in Chicago. The city's longtime Democratic mayor, Ed Kelly, was also a close family friend, though that didn't stop Edith from also inviting whichever Republican happened to occupy the Illinois governor's mansion to dinner.

According to classmates at the Girls Latin School, Nancy was charming and full of personality, popular with the boys, at ease with grownups, and loved to sing and dance. By her college years she had also developed a style of her own, and a rather proper style it was. Mike Wallace, who got to know the family when he was starting out at a Chicago radio station in the early 1940s, described her as "very ladylike, a Smith girl, with the Peter Pan collar and the black patent leather shoes and the white gloves and the pearls." Shortly after moving to Los Angeles in 1949, under contract to MGM, she met a fledging fashion designer James Galanos, and began buying his dresses at half-price sales at the end of the season. "I remember the first dress of Jimmy's that I got," Mrs. Reagan has said. "I was so excited about it. It was black with a white collar and white cuffs."

Two decades later, when Ronald Reagan was elected governor, she would call upon Galanos to design the first of four inaugural gowns, a one-shouldered white sheath. She would order something quite similar when her husband was elected president. "I have to say one thing about Nancy," Galanos told one of her biographers. "She was very definite about whether she liked something or not. If I put something on her and said, 'I think you look perfect in that,' and it was something different from her usual look, she'd say, 'Well, yes, it's nice, but I don't know.' Once she started like that, I knew she wasn't going to be happy in it. So I just followed. I would suggest. I would show her. She knew, really, how she wanted to look. And, I must say, she was right."

And how perfect she looked each time, so slim and soigné in her white Galanos gown, dancing with her tall and handsome husband, in his tuxedo or white tie and tails, the two of them an inspiring picture of marital fidelity and happiness.

For when all is said and done, the role that meant the most to her was wife. It was who she was and all she wanted to be: Mrs. Ronald Reagan. As important and gratifying as the various duties and projects she took on as first lady were to her, they were subordinate to her essential mission. For Nancy Reagan, the best way to serve her country was to take good care of its commander in chief. In a literal, physical sense, she nursed him back to health three times in eight years, after the assassination attempt and two cancer operations. Otherwise, she went on doing what she had been doing since they wed in 1952, being Ronnie's protector, helpmate, morale booster, antennae, personnel director, crisis manager, trusted adviser, and loving spouse. Perhaps former CIA director Richard Helms, a man she considered one of her closest confidantes, said it best: "Nancy Reagan was *totally* devoted to Ronald Reagan and his causes. She was just keeping track of everything that was going on with respect to Ronnie—who was undermining him, who was supporting him. I don't know how any first lady could have been any closer to her president than she was."

The governor with the first lady of California, who is dressed in a one-shouldered Galanos gown with embroidered daisies, at the first gubernatorial ball on January 2, 1967.

# LIFE BEFORE
# THE WHITE HOUSE

### 1921–1980

*Extraordinarily beautiful . . . Nancy's face, which has every right*
*to be bold and assertive has instead a soft dreamy quality.*
*Add to this a figure of "oomph!" You'd be crazy about the child.*

— ALLA NAZIMOVA, 1940, GODMOTHER TO NANCY DAVIS

Capturing the essence of young Nancy Davis, these vivid observations fore-shadow an extraordinary life filled with beauty and "oomph." What emerges from the essential elements of her childhood is the portrait of a great lady. Not just a first lady, but a woman of dignity, grace, and devotion.

Born in New York, Nancy spent her early life in Chicago as the daughter of an exuberant mother and a highly respected neurosurgeon. Inspired by the loving marriage of Edith and Loyal Davis, she flourished. Many say this was the model for her own successful relationship, as it provided a vivid example of the true meaning of love. Along the way, her mother's colorful humor, sparkling personality and classic sense of style became a part of Nancy's spirit. A family friend aptly described Edith: "Her face was beautiful, a classic face; her smile warmed the eye and the heart of the beholder. Her hair, under her Bes-Ben hat had begun to gray. She wore a smartly tailored suit, white kid gloves, mid-heel pumps. . . ."

Complementing her mother's charm, her father's discipline and desire to succeed shaped Nancy's character. And it is no surprise to learn that Nancy Davis's early sophistication is recorded in her 1939 yearbook upon graduation from the Girls Latin School. "Nancy's social perfection is a constant source of amazement.

Ronald and Nancy Reagan at the Academy Awards in the 1950s.
OPPOSITE: The engaged couple in a Hollywood publicity photo from 1952.
PAGE 24: California's first lady in the 1960s.

She is invariably becomingly and suitably dressed." When introduced to society, Nancy Davis made her debut wearing "a single strand of pearls, which she wore with her silver-trimmed white gown."

How did a girl from Smith College with pearls and evening gowns find her way to Hollywood? With a phone call from family friend Spencer Tracy, a screen test was arranged at MGM after Tracy encouraged George Cukor to give her a chance. With confidence and courage in hand, she signed a seven-year contract with MGM in 1949. She was beside herself "with excitement" as this "marked the end of one period of life and the beginning of another."

Soon after, Nancy Davis met Ronald Reagan on a blind date in the fall of 1949. Well, not so blind for her, since she had already seen "Ronnie" in pictures and was delighted to learn he looked as good in person as he did on screen. Relying on her preference for classic elegance, she wore a sharp, shapely black dress with a crisp white collar. What did he see? "The door opened," the young suitor wrote, "not on the expected fan magazine version of a starlet, but on a small, slender young lady with dark hair and a wide-spaced pair of hazel eyes that looked right at you and made you look back."

On March 4, 1952, at the Little Brown Church in Studio City, California, Ronald Reagan and Nancy Davis were married. With the birth of their daughter, Patti, and son, Ron, Nancy Reagan tended the home fires while her husband hosted the televised General Electric Theater and went on the road for extended periods of time, as spokesman for his employer. When away, he wrote, "I love you so very much. I don't even mind that life made me wait so long to find you. The waiting only made the finding sweeter."

Weekends at their Malibu Canyon ranch made life even better. It was where they had courted, where Nancy got to know Ronnie's children Maureen and Michael, and, finally, where they took Patti and Ron on weekends.

And sweeter it became on a mountaintop in the Pacific Palisades when General Electric built the "House of the Future" for Ronnie and Nancy Reagan. Dedicated to making a beautiful home, Nancy employed her palette of buttercup yellows, pale peaches, and bright persimmon reds to warm their contemporary surroundings. For the next twenty-seven years, their good friends would meet at that house to talk politics, ultimately becoming the famous "Kitchen Cabinet."

In October 1964 Ronald Reagan, the young G.E. spokesman, delivered a speech entitled "A Time for Choosing" over national television on Barry Goldwater's behalf. As the saying goes, a new political star was born. Reagan's powerful rhetoric

*I've said it before and I'll say it once again:*
*my life didn't begin until I met Ronnie.*

— NANCY REAGAN

The Reagans at their "Yearling Row" ranch during the 1950s.

and captivating delivery electrified the audience: "Either we believe in our traditional system of individual liberty or we abandon the American Revolution and confess that an intellectual elite in a far distant capital can plan our lives for us better than we plan them ourselves."

Reflecting on this historic moment, Nancy Reagan said, "Ronnie always believed that we're all put here for a purpose. We might not know why or what the purpose is, but eventually we will. Barry opened the door. And then Ronnie took it along."

Straight to Sacramento is where he took it. He found his true calling in politics and so did she. "She didn't know what she was getting into, I don't think," said political strategist Stu Spencer. "But it turned out Nancy was born a politician. They were a team. . . . Her own political skills were better, in terms of what was best for Ron, than even his own. . . . I've always said he'd never have made it without her."

She stood by her husband's side as he announced his candidacy for governor, and joined him through all the challenges of his first gubernatorial bid. "Our problems are many," the candidate Reagan said, "but our capacity for solving them is immense."

The Reagans enjoy a boat ride while visiting Newport Beach, California, in 1964.

After spending election night at the home of their good friends Marion and Earle Jorgensen, the Reagans learned of their victory, carrying all but three counties. The next evening Earle Jorgensen toasted, "To the Governor! Who knows, one day he may be our president."

As Nancy Reagan embraced the challenges of being California's first lady, she learned that the media scrutinized every move she made. "Politics is a completely different life," she said. "In politics, you aren't protected in any way. You don't belong for a night to a theater audience; you belong to everyone all the time."

During that same period, she visited American soldiers in veterans' hospitals who had been wounded in Vietnam. Her concern expanded into a program for returning POWs, which consisted of several dinners held in their honor. "The first dinner in Sacramento was an unforgettable experience for Ronnie and me," she wrote, "and when Commander Charles Southwick presented me with the tin spoon he had eaten with during his seven years of captivity, I was in tears again." In her opinion, the return of the POWs marked the high point of their Sacramento years.

As their first gubernatorial term drew to a close, 1968 marked the first presidential run by Ronald Reagan. While she did not think this was the time, Nancy Reagan supported her husband's decision. As she told the *Washington Post*, "I think it is important for a man to do something about the things he feels strongly about. Whatever satisfies and fulfills him makes for a better marriage." Despite abandoning presidential aspirations, 1968 ended on a high note for the Reagans when the *Los Angeles Times* named Nancy Reagan "Woman of the Year." The *Times* wrote, "Nancy Reagan treaded the intricate paths of politics, state and national, with never a misstep," and commended her for doing "a job few women would envy for long if they understood the day in, day out grind that ceremonial duties can become. She was poised, friendly, informed, interested and beautifully turned out day after day, not just when she felt like it." During the same period, she was named to the International Best Dressed List for the first time. After receiving the same recognition for several years, she was elevated to the Hall of Fame.

On January 4, 1971, her husband was sworn in for a second term as governor of California, and during this time Richard Nixon dispatched the engaging governor and his charming wife to all points around the globe. With trips to Japan, Thailand, Singapore, and South Korea, their goal was to reassure our allies that Nixon's historic meeting with China would not change their relationships with the United States.

Nineteen-seventy-four marked their last full year in Sacramento. When asked what was ahead, she replied, "We'll take that day by day." Their new ranch in Santa

Barbara became a fulfilling escape for the Reagans. It was a modest but charming retreat as they transitioned into one of the most challenging periods of their lives.

And still, Ronald and Nancy Reagan did not let any grass grow under their political feet. "Of Ronnie's five campaigns for public office, the one I remember most vividly is the only one he lost. That was in 1976 when he challenged President Gerald Ford for the Republican nomination. That campaign was so exciting, so dramatic, and so emotional that in my mind, it almost overshadows Ronnie's four victories." Struggling with fund-raising problems, the "little campaign that could" forged through every primary, engaging support across the country, but ultimately conceded to incumbent President Ford. Nancy Reagan lovingly reassured her husband, "In all the years we've been married, you have never done anything to disappoint me. And I've never been prouder of you than I am now." Despite the loss, Ronald Reagan continued to express his beliefs to the American people, with Nancy at his side all the way. The next presidential election campaign was only four years away.

On Election Day in 1980, they voted at the same house they had voted at during the past twenty-five years. Nancy Reagan's husband claimed he voted for her. As was the tradition, they went to the Jorgensens' for dinner, but this time arrived via an enormous motorcade because by 5:15 p.m. PST, Ronald Reagan had been declared the winner. "Congratulations honey," she said, as she hugged the fortieth president of the United States.

ABOVE: The governor and first lady of California address the public.
OPPOSITE: The Reagans in the living room of their home in Pacific Palisades.

**THE WEDDING** "I remember the morning of our wedding day so well. At my apartment in Westwood, I got dressed in the wedding suit that I'd chosen from I. Magnin's: A gray wool suit with a white collar, which I wore with a small flowered hat with a veil." Tailored, crisp, and classic, this wedding suit was a reflection of Nancy Reagan's elegant taste. On the morning of March 4, 1952, Ronald Reagan arrived at his bride's apartment with her bridal bouquet in hand, and together they rode to the Little Brown Church in the valley. The ceremony was small and subdued, but Nancy Reagan's ebullience made up for any lack of fanfare. Reflecting on that special day, she recalled, "I was in a happy fog. . . . I missed it altogether when the minister said what I most wanted to hear: 'I now pronounce you man and wife.'" Their intimate wedding marked the beginning of what has been observed by many as a remarkable love story.

LEFT: The newlyweds exchange wedding rings on March 4, 1952.

RIGHT: Wool basketweave suit with a cotton pique collar and turned cuffs. The label reads: "Manor-Bourne Exclusive with I. Magnin and Company."

OPPOSITE: Detail of the collar.

*I love you so much—I never thought I could love you
more than the day we were married but I do.*

— NANCY REAGAN, 1967 ANNIVERSARY LETTER

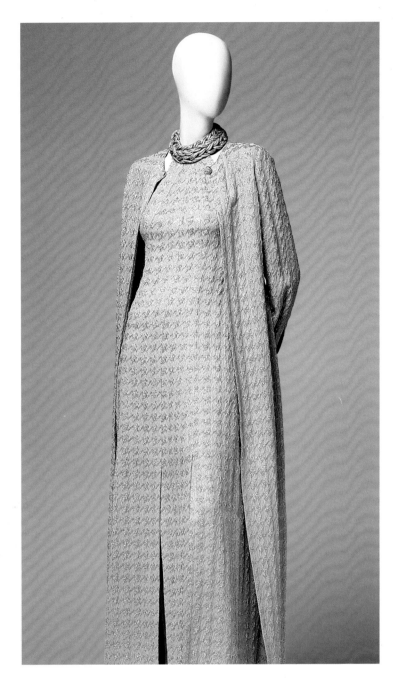

**THE SECOND GUBERNATORIAL INAUGURATION**    By the time Ronald Reagan was inaugurated governor of California for the second time, on January 4, 1971, some may have expected the attention paid to the clothes of the state's first lady to have been old news. Four years had passed since Nancy Reagan caused a sensation at the first inaugural ball in a one-shouldered white Galanos gown sprinkled with diamante daisies. However, Californians remained as excited to see what their first lady was wearing as they were to hear the governor's address. Mrs. Reagan wore this striking brocade gown to the second inaugural ball. For this design, she had called upon her old friend James Galanos, who went on to create all of Nancy Reagan's inaugural gowns.

LEFT: Brocade evening gown with a braided halter neckline and matching coat, designed by James Galanos for Amelia Gray's boutique.

RIGHT: Detail of the neckline with jeweled button.

OPPOSITE: Governor and Mrs. Reagan in their Pacific Palisades home in 1971.

*I don't know of any clothes that were made as well Jimmy's—you could almost wear them inside out. The fabric was great. Everything about them was so special.*

— NANCY REAGAN

Mrs. Reagan wore this gown many years after she acquired it, when she and the governor visited Vice President Spiro Theodore Agnew for a Governors Dinner on February 24, 1972, at the State Department.

OPPOSITE LEFT: Bugle-beaded sheath with a beaded hem, designed by James Galanos for Amelia Gray's boutique.

OPPOSITE RIGHT: Detail of the beaded hemline.

**DESIGNS BY JAMES GALANOS**   After young Nancy Davis arrived in Hollywood, a girlfriend in the publicity department of MGM brought her to Amelia Gray's fashionable boutique in Beverly Hills. Gray immediately took a liking to the outgoing actress. And it was she who introduced Nancy to the stylish creations of James Galanos. At the time, Mr. Galanos sold his designs exclusively through Gray's upscale boutique. He delivered his clothes in person, and he fondly recalled visiting the shop when Nancy was there too. "From there on, there was a nice relationship between the three of us. And so whenever Nancy needed something special, she'd call Amelia or me," Mr. Galanos recounted. This beaded sheath was designed by Mr. Galanos for Amelia Gray and dates to the 1950s.

*My memory of the 1980 campaign is just a big blur. I remember sinking into bed at night, absolutely exhausted.*

— NANCY REAGAN

Supported by his wife and family, Ronald Reagan announces his candidacy for president of the United States in 1979.

OPPOSITE: Two-piece velvet cocktail suit and satin camisole, designed by Adolfo.

**RUNNING FOR PRESIDENT**   When Ronald Reagan announced his run for the presidency in New York on November 13, 1979, Nancy Reagan stood by his side in this velvet Adolfo suit. The 1980 campaign was an arduous one, and Mrs. Reagan was a tireless campaigner. She trekked the campaign trail with her husband, hosted cocktails and dinners, and even took trips of her own to speak on his behalf. Her dedication to all five of her husband's campaigns never wavered, and she remained his biggest champion. Mrs. Reagan wore this suit again as first lady, on February 10, 1981, to the performance of the Dance Theatre of Harlem at the Kennedy Center. The suit's lines are so classic that she was able to wear it again after the presidency, in 1992 and 2003.

# WHITE HOUSE
# BEGINNINGS

*I threw myself into these various first lady roles — spokeswoman, hostess, manager, and friend. I thought all of them were important. But there was one part of the job that outranked them all. Above everything else, the first lady is the president's wife.*

— NANCY REAGAN

Imagine what a thrill it must be to know your new residence is 1600 Pennsylvania Avenue. Yet, for twenty-seven years, the Reagans made their home at 1669 San Onofre in Pacific Palisades. As a sign of his devotion to his wife, Ronald Reagan had drawn a little heart with their initials in wet cement on the patio off their bedroom. Thus, moving to Washington was bittersweet, as San Onofre, the sentimental choice, was up for sale.

Coming off the trails of an intense campaign, there was no time for rest. Ronald Reagan was assembling his team and creating a plan for the first ninety days in office, while Nancy Reagan prepared for a cumbersome, complicated move to a residence she had not seen.

A few weeks after the election, Rosalyn Carter invited Nancy Reagan to the White House so she could get a behind-the-scenes view of what was to come. The interiors had not been renovated since the Kennedy administration. Mrs. Reagan remarked, "On that first visit, my overall feeling was of surprise that the residence looked so dreary and uninviting. . . . Frankly, the White House was run-down and a bit shabby." While she privately resolved to fix it up once she got to Washington, she was tasked with orchestrating a move across the continent, with a target date of January 14, six days before the inauguration.

First Lady Nancy Reagan at the inaugural ball on January 20, 1981.

OPPOSITE: Nancy Reagan in the Red Room of the White House, wearing the satin ball gown and beaded lace overlay that James Galanos designed for the 1981 inauguration. The gown is now in the Smithsonian Institution.

PAGE 42: Tulips on the South Lawn of the White House.

Home base became Blair House, the president's official guest house, which also needed attention. While unpacking, Nancy Reagan worried about all their personal belongings being shipped to White House storage for delivery on Inauguration Day. While her husband was busy with meetings, over a six-day period, she began the difficult task of assembling a professional staff: chief of staff, social secretary, and press secretary, among others. Family members from across the country arrived, celebrations began, and an inaugural gala to fete Ronald and Nancy Reagan was staged by Frank Sinatra, Ethel Merman, Bob Hope, Rich Little, Donny Osmond, and Johnny Carson. The next day was the inauguration.

Rising early, Nancy Reagan prepared for a full slate of activities. At the ceremony, as she walked toward the audience, she caught the eye of her friend Betsy Bloomingdale. "I know we were both thinking the same thought," she observed when she saw Betsy's face, "from now on it would never be the same again."

Holding the Reagan family bible, Nancy Reagan stood beside her husband as he took the oath of office. As he raised his hand, "The dark cloudy sky over his head began to part slightly, within seconds there was a gaping hole in the gray overcast and a brilliant golden shaft of wintery sun burst through the clouds," *Time* magazine reported. "Maybe this is an omen," Nancy Reagan wondered, "maybe it was meant to be."

Overcome with joy, she listened to her husband's first inaugural address. "I will work, I will save, I will sacrifice, I will endure, I will fight cheerfully and do my utmost, as if the issue of the whole struggle depended on me alone."

During lunch at the Capitol, Ronald Reagan announced that the planes bearing American hostages left Iranian airspace and were free of Iran. From one intense moment to the next, President and Mrs. Reagan were off to the inaugural parade. All Americans who watched were captivated by their first lady. She was extraordinarily photogenic, with striking good looks and refined stylishness.

The media hailed the inaugural festivities and got down to business moments after the parties were over. Fatigued by a year of critical press, Nancy Reagan took matters into her own hands and "made a fresh start with the Washington press corps," by appearing at the Gridiron Dinner dressed in rummage-sale leftovers and singing a spoof on "Second Hand Rose" entitled "Second Hand Clothes." The headlines were fabulous: "First Lady Floors 'Em with Song and Dance" and "She Sings, She Jokes, She's a Hit." Even the *Washington Post* documented the moment: "A number of those image-makers left the ballroom saying that Nancy Reagan's song and dance number had transformed her image."

The western facade of the U.S. Capitol on inauguration day, January 20, 1981.

By 1983, the possibility of another presidential campaign was looming. According to Nancy Reagan, "Had it been up to me, Ronald Reagan might well have been a one-term president." She feared for her husband's safety because of the assassination attempt but respected his decision to run. "Campaigns are never pleasant, and this one was no exception," she wrote.

This time the opponent was Walter Mondale, who proved to be a formidable foe. After stumbling in his first debate, Ronald Reagan recovered handsomely in the next. On election night, the Reagans were at the Jorgensens' home once again, and within hours of the polls closing, a landslide victory celebration was underway. "Ronnie won every state except Minnesota and the District of Columbia," Nancy proudly wrote.

Of course, the second inauguration would be considerably easier than the first. No move. No new staff. No new agenda. The wheels were immediately in motion as she prepared for two ceremonies because January 20 fell on a Sunday; ultimately, the public ceremony on Monday had to be moved indoors due to bitterly cold weather.

Listening to her husband deliver his second inaugural address, Nancy Reagan was moved to tears when his inspiring words echoed their own personal journey to the White House: "We believed then and now: There are no limits to growth and human progress when men and women are free to follow their dreams."

Mrs. Reagan waves to the president on the monitor behind her during the First Lady Tribute at the Republican National Convention in Texas on August 22, 1984.
OPPOSITE: President and Mrs. Reagan exit the stage at the Dallas Convention Center. President Reagan had just accepted the 1984 Republican nomination.

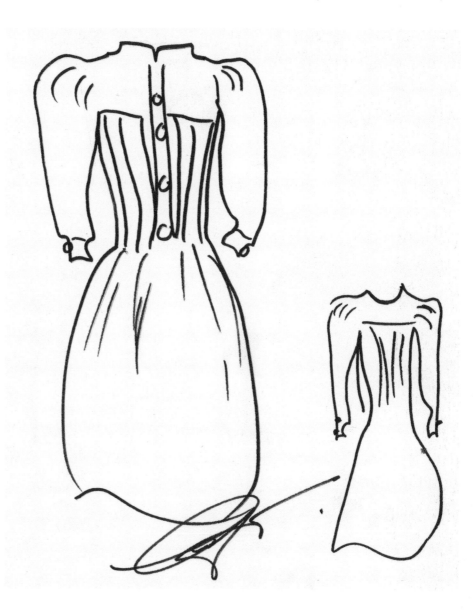

*For the first inauguration, she decided to use red, which would be a focus point, because most of the audience would be wearing dark-colored clothing. At the second ceremony, we used a bright blue color, again, creating a nice contrast from the dark colors that would be surrounding her.*

— ADOLFO, 2007

Front and back sketches of the inauguration coat, signed by Adolfo.

OPPOSITE: Wool crepe day dress with matching twill coat and hat, designed by Adolfo.

**THE FIRST PRESIDENTIAL INAUGURATION** On January 20, 1981, Nancy Reagan accompanied her husband to St. John's Episcopal Church in this custom-made red day dress, coat, and hat designed by Adolfo. After services, the Reagans joined the Carters and the Mondales at the White House, and together they rode to the Capitol for the inauguration ceremony. With the Capitol adorned in red, white, and blue and the U.S. Marine Band poised to play, Nancy Reagan watched her husband be sworn into office. "Then, suddenly, it was over. The president kissed me, and a booming twenty-one-gun salute rang out in honor of the new president," she recalled. As the echoes of the salute grew soft, President Ronald Reagan gave his optimistic inaugural speech. The visual splendor of that 1981 ceremony was memorable, and just a mere glimmer of the dignity and formality that Nancy Reagan would bring to the White House thereafter.

Nancy Reagan watches her husband take the oath of office, administered by Chief Justice Warren Burger.

RIGHT: Officially the president of the United States, Ronald Reagan gives his wife a kiss.

The president and first lady wave
to cheering onlookers as the
inaugural parade escorts them from
the Capitol to the White House.

*When I accepted this beautiful dress made by Mr. Galanos, I did so with the hope that it would spotlight the American fashion industry and with the hope that it would be a valuable reflection of my own time.*

— NANCY REAGAN, 1981

**THE 1981 INAUGURAL BALLS**   On the evening of January 20, President and Mrs. Reagan attended a record-setting ten inaugural balls. And Nancy Reagan garnered much of the press, once again, for her dramatic inaugural gown. This one-shouldered satin dress with an embroidered overlay and satin cloak with a gathered collar were designed exclusively for her by Galanos. Although the dress's silhouette was simple, its hand-embroidered beading in a fernlike pattern was a work of art, having taken more than four weeks to craft. "I loved it, and I wore it proudly," she said.

The Reagans were finally able to enjoy their first dance as president and first lady at the tenth ball of the evening. As Tommy Dorsey's Orchestra played "You'll Never Know," the president of the United States took his wife in his arms and spun her gracefully around the stage at the Shoreham Hotel.

The first lady wore this gown just once more a few weeks later, to the White House reception for the diplomatic corps. Shortly thereafter, it was donated to the Smithsonian Institution.

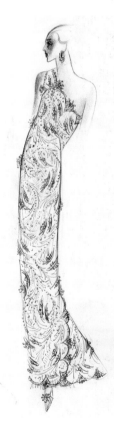

OPPOSITE: Satin cloak with gathered collar and tie closure, designed by James Galanos.

LEFT: Detail of the gathered collar.

ABOVE: Drawings by James Galanos of the satin cloak and inaugural gown.

*She's representing
the highest office in the
country, in the world. . . .
I just wanted her to look
elegant and in keeping
with the new formality.*

— JAMES GALANOS, 1981

LEFT: The first lady shares a few words with guests at the Shoreham Hotel's inaugural ball.

BELOW: A Reagan family portrait, taken in the Red Room on January 20, 1981.

OPPOSITE: President and Mrs. Reagan en route to the evening's inaugural balls.

President and Mrs. Reagan on
election night at the Century Plaza
Hotel in Los Angeles.

RIGHT: Printed silk cocktail dress
with ribbon sash, designed by
James Galanos.

**ELECTION NIGHT, 1984**   This simple dress, with little stars, polka dots, and a
black bow-tie sash, reflected the buoyancy felt among Reagan's supporters on
election night, November 6, 1984. The optimism for which President Reagan was
so well known was certainly in the air that night, and the incumbent president
received overwhelming support. Nancy Reagan recalled, "We expected a victory, but
we weren't prepared for a landslide." She and the president followed the election
results on television with friends in their home state of California. Upon hearing
the news, they joyfully made their way to the Century Plaza Hotel for the president's
acceptance speech.

President Reagan concludes his victory speech at the Century Plaza Hotel.

President and Mrs. Reagan
enjoy the inaugural gala at the
Washington Convention Center.

LEFT: A White House press announcement features a drawing of the silk crepe gown designed for the inaugural gala, signed "To Nancy Reagan by Bill Blass."

RIGHT: The president and first lady at the inaugural gala.

**THE SECOND INAUGURAL GALA**   A shower of fireworks over the North Lawn of the White House ignited the week's inaugural events. On the following night, Saturday, January 19, the 1985 inaugural gala was held at the Washington Convention Center. Frank Sinatra hosted the star-studded celebration, with tributes and performances by Mikhail Baryshnikov, Elizabeth Taylor, Rich Little, Dean Martin, and Donna Summer. To this jubilant affair, Mrs. Reagan wore a red silk gown designed by Bill Blass and an elegant five-strand pearl choker.

As she had done in 1981, Nancy Reagan relied upon a triumvirate of American designers to craft her dresses for the public events of the 1985 inaugural week. The theme was patriotic: Blass, Galanos, and Adolfo dressed the first lady in red, white, and blue, respectively.

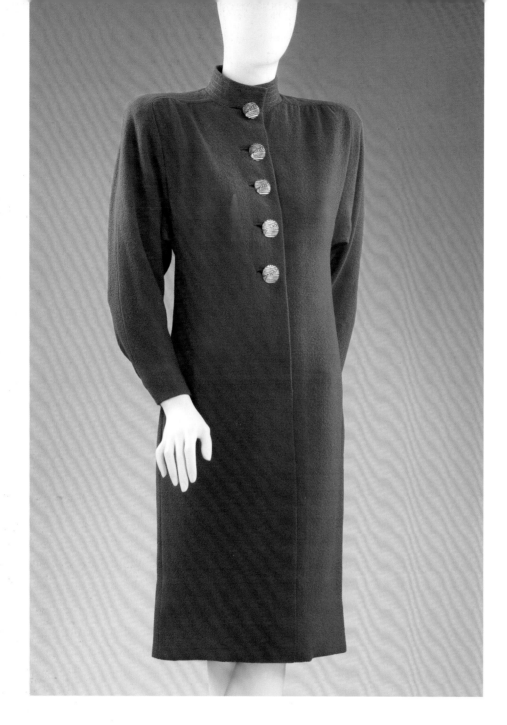

**THE PRIVATE INAUGURATION** Attired in this red day dress designed by Galanos, Nancy Reagan accompanied her husband to St. John's Episcopal Church, just as she had on the day of his first inauguration. And once again, she held the bible that had belonged to her mother-in-law, Nelle, while her husband was sworn into office as the president of the United States. However, that is where the similarities to the first inauguration ended. Since January 20 was a Sunday, a private oath was administered that day, in an intimate ceremony before an audience of eighty on the Grand Staircase landing of the White House. At a modest celebration that night at the White House, President and Mrs. Reagan thanked the entertainers who had honored them at the previous night's gala. The night would be an early one, however, because the next day called for a repeat performance, with the president taking the oath in a public ceremony at the United States Capitol.

Wool crepe day dress with standing collar, designed by James Galanos.

OPPOSITE: Ronald Reagan being sworn into office for a second term, in a private ceremony at the White House on Sunday, January 20, 1985.

**THE PUBLIC INAUGURATION**   In 1985 President Reagan was sworn into office for a second time, on January 21, in a public ceremony at the Capitol. In her blue Adolfo dress, Nancy Reagan stood by his side, attentive to the protocol at hand. That year, the weather was so bitter cold that the ceremony had to be moved indoors. It was held, for the first time in history, in the rotunda of the Capitol.

Unfortunately, doctors predicted frostbite for the high-school bands that had come to escort the president and first lady from the Capitol to the White House. So, with sadness, the parade was cancelled, and festivities convened inside the Capital Centre. Standing on a float that resembled the American flag, Mrs. Reagan expressed her gratitude to the disappointed band members, and then took her seat. Almost immediately, she bounced back up to the podium. "I forgot something. I was supposed to introduce my roommate," she said apologetically. This prompted a humorous reply from her "roommate," the president, "How could you have forgotten me?" They both received thunderous applause.

The public inauguration ceremony was held on Monday, January 21, 1985, inside the Capitol.

OPPOSITE: Wool crepe day dress with chain belt and matching Melton overcoat and hat, designed by Adolfo.

Detail of the dress and coat lapel.

*We felt so bad for all the kids who had saved their money to come to Washington to play that we found a place to have them perform indoors instead.*

— NANCY REAGAN

The Reagans wave from the float
in the Capital Centre.

**THE SECOND INAUGURAL BALLS**   An estimated 50,000 people came out to support President and Mrs. Reagan at the nine inaugural balls held in their honor on January 21, 1985. Again, Nancy Reagan wore a shimmering Galanos gown, beaded from top to bottom. The one-piece bolero and midriff was hand-embroidered in an Art Deco pattern with satin bugle beads, stones, and faux jewels. A vermicelli pattern accented with crystals swirled along the skirt. This time around, the president and first lady made sure they shared a dance together before the end of the night. The celebration began at the Young Americans Ball, where President Reagan embraced his wife and led her around the floor to a rendition of "Tennessee Waltz."

Mrs. Reagan wore this gown again to a White House dinner she hosted for Prince Charles and Princess Diana in 1985.

Nancy Reagan on stage at the John F. Kennedy Center's inaugural ball.

OPPOSITE: Beaded ball gown with a two-piece effect, featuring a short bolero over a fitted midriff, designed by James Galanos.

Detail of the bolero and midriff.

The Reagans share their first
dance at the Inaugural Ball for
Young Americans.

The president invites his wife to
dance again at the eighth ball of the
evening, at the Shoreham Hotel.

**1982 GRIDIRON DINNER** The Gridiron Dinner on March 27, 1982, marked a high point in the public perception of Nancy Reagan's style. The first lady surprised her husband and an audience of 600 of the most influential publishers, political columnists, and Washington journalists, when she walked on stage dressed in a mismatched outfit and feathered hat. She titled the song to her skit "Secondhand Clothes," and, in lyrics set to the tune of "Secondhand Rose," she mocked the media's rebukes of her. In a dramatic closing, she smashed a replica plate from the new White House china set on the stage floor. After this pivotal moment, the press turned from criticism of Mrs. Reagan's style to flattery.

An outfit composed of a feathered hat with crinoline veil, a polka-dot blouse, a floral smock, a floral printed skirt, and rubber Wellingtons, accessorized with a marabou boa and opera pearls.

Mrs. Reagan heads for the stage
at the Gridiron Dinner to
perform her surprise skit entitled
"Secondhand Clothes."

# A NATION
# COMES TOGETHER

# SOMBER MOMENTS

*With us here today are families of the eight heroic men who gave their lives in the attempt to affect your rescue. "Greater glory hath no man than that he lay down his life for another."*

— RONALD REAGAN, JANUARY 27, 1981

With heartfelt sorrow, the first lady lamented, "There seemed to be so many of these sad times" during her eight years in Washington.

A week after the 1981 inauguration, Nancy and Ronald Reagan welcomed home the fifty-two hostages who had been held in Iran and celebrated by lighting the national Christmas tree, which had been extinguished during their captivity. It was a happy moment tempered by sadness.

The new president and his first lady met with the families privately, including the families of the eight men who had lost their lives during the earlier, unsuccess-

Mrs. Reagan visits Omaha Beach in Normandy, France,
for the D-Day memorial ceremony on June 6, 1982.
OPPOSITE: After the ceremony, Mrs. Reagan places flowers on
the grave of Elizabeth Richardson, an American Red Cross worker.
PAGE 74: The Festival of the Fourth on July 3, 1987, kicks off
the nation's Independence Day festivities at the Jefferson Memorial.

ful attempt to rescue the hostages. A public ceremony in their honor was held on the South Lawn of the White House, and, as the President and Mrs. Reagan walked away, they knew it would not be the last time they would try to console the relatives of men and women who died in the service of their country.

In October 1983, the Reagans received news that 241 marines had died as they slept, resting from the duties of trying to keep the peace in Lebanon. "Nancy and I were in a state of grief," the president wrote. On a Friday morning in November, they flew to Camp Lejeune in North Carolina for a service honoring the soldiers killed in Lebanon and Grenada. "We would go to see [the families]. He would hug them . . . I would hug them," remembers Nancy Reagan. "And,

On January 27, 1981, President and Mrs. Reagan welcome home the fifty-two hostages who had been held captive in Iran for 444 days and also honor the courage of the eight men who lost their lives in an earlier failed rescue attempt.

really, all that you could do was hug them and say how sorry you were. It was very hard for everybody."

Proudly, Nancy Reagan stood by her husband as he presided over the dedication of the Vietnam Veterans Memorial in November 1984. "I spent a lot of time in veterans' hospitals, visiting American soldiers who had been wounded in Vietnam," she sadly recounted. "If you ever start feeling sorry for yourself, try visiting hospitals." Echoing her concern for these dedicated Americans, her husband saluted the soldiers by saying, "They were both our children and our heroes. We will never ever forget them. We will never forget their devotion and their sacrifice. They stand before us, marching into time and into shared memory, forever. May God bless their souls."

At Andrews Air Force Base on April 23, 1983, President and Mrs. Reagan view
the caskets of Americans who died in the suicide bombing of the U.S. Embassy five days
earlier in Beirut, Lebanon. They could not foresee the devastation the nation would endure
a few months later, when the U.S. Marine barracks in Lebanon were bombed.

*And we have held and spoken with those who have faced hardship or known great tragedy. On those occasions, the strength, faith, hope, and perseverance that seem uniquely American find new definition.*

— PRESIDENT AND MRS. REAGAN, JUNE 28, 1986

Continuing to honor those who gave their lives in defense of freedom, Nancy Reagan traveled to Europe with her husband for the forty-year anniversary of the D-Day invasion in June 1984. "The first stop was Pointe du Hoc," she recalled, "where American Rangers . . . had overcome enormous German resistance and climbed a sheer hundred foot cliff . . . more than 100 died." It was a terribly emotional experience, as the president's words paid tribute to their efforts: "These are the boys of Pointe du Hoc. These are the men who took the cliffs. These are the champions who helped free a continent. These are the heroes who helped end a war." Following this historical speech, they flew to Omaha Beach, "which was a heartbreaker," remembers Nancy, "the sight of endless rows of white crosses and stars of David—more than nine thousand of them and they represented only a portion of the casualties of D-Day."

At times, Nancy Reagan admired her husband's eternal optimism. "Anyone can be optimistic when times are good, but Ronnie remains hopeful even in the worst of times." Recalling the tragedy of the *Challenger* in January 1986, she admired how he could reassure the nation that seven astronauts had not died in vain, and that this tragedy would not mark the end of America's scientific progress. "The future doesn't belong to the fainthearted; it belongs to the brave," her husband courageously reminded a mourning nation.

The Reagans join with family members of the astronauts whose lives were lost on the Space Shuttle *Challenger* at the memorial service in Houston, Texas, on January 31, 1986.
OPPOSITE: President and Mrs. Reagan visit the Vietnam Memorial on Veteran's Day, November 11, 1988, four years after they first dedicated the monument.

# CELEBRATIONS

*America was ready for a party.*

— *TIME*, JANUARY 1981

The first inhabitants of the White House were John and Abigail Adams. When they moved in during November 1800, the paint was still wet. Since then, Americans have looked to the White House as a symbol of inspiration in times of uncertainty and of celebration in times of joy.

As first lady, Nancy Reagan embraced the task of creating memorable celebrations. She started by enhancing and expanding the traditional Easter Egg Roll event, which began in 1878 when President Rutherford B. Hayes invited rowdy "Easter Egg Rollers" onto the White House Lawn.

When it came to celebrations, the president's personal favorite was the Fourth of July, Independence Day, which also falls within two days of Nancy Reagan's birthday. Back in 1776, John Adams wrote his wife, Abigail, that the anniversary of our independence should be observed with great fanfare: "[W]ith pomp and parades . . . shows and games . . . and sports and guns and bells . . . with bonfires and illuminations, from one end of this continent to the other, and from this time forevermore." As president and first lady, the Reagans gladly executed this charge, beginning with the formation of a commission in 1982 to restore the Statue of Liberty and Ellis Island by July 4, 1986, Lady Liberty's centennial.

On July 3, 1986, the unveiling of Lady Liberty took place, followed by spectacular ceremonies across the nation. The president told the American people, with his beloved Nancy at his side, "And which of us does not think of other grandfathers and grandmothers from so many places around the globe, for whom this statue was the first glimpse of America?" On July 5, Nancy Reagan, accompanied by 100 French and American schoolchildren, officially opened Liberty Island, becoming the first official tourists to climb inside the newly renovated statue.

On July 3, 1987, she stood by her husband's side at the Jefferson Memorial as he announced America's Economic Bill of Rights and said, "We're still Jefferson's children, still believers that freedom is the unalienable right of all of God's children."

Every year ended in great style with the festivities of Christmas. Thoughtfully, President and Mrs. Reagan would stay in Washington so that their Secret Service agents would not have to leave their families. For their first Christmas in 1981, the Reagans were forced to activate the lights on the national Christmas tree remotely

Fireworks rain over the White House.

from the East Room in the White House due to security concerns. In December 1984, Nancy Reagan was thrilled to be able to light the tree from the South Portico of the White House. The president, in a spirited address, said, "And do you know what? I've talked myself into the Christmas spirit. I'm going to give a gift right now. I'm not going to light the tree; I'm going to let Nancy do it. Where's the button?"

The 1988 Easter Egg Roll on the South Lawn.
OPPOSITE: The White House Rose Garden in bloom outside the Oval Office.

**EASTER AT THE WHITE HOUSE**   In this smart two-piece Bill Blass ensemble, Nancy Reagan greeted the American Egg Board at the White House on March 25, 1988. Every year, the American Egg Board donated dozens of hard-boiled eggs for the Easter Egg Roll on the White House Lawn, and this year, they came with a special gift: a decorative egg with a pierced design of roses and an American flag.

By 1988, Easter at the White House was quite an attraction. On public display were what came to be known as the Nancy Reagan White House Easter Egg Collection—little wooden eggs painted by the nation's foremost artists and illustrators—which she introduced in 1981 and augmented each year. Children hunted for eggs while clowns and cartoon characters roamed the lawn, handing out balloons and eggs autographed by celebrities. The Easter Bunny and live entertainment kept the festivities going for hours. It was estimated that, by 1988, Nancy Reagan's Easter Egg Roll attracted 35,000 visitors to the White House.

The National Egg Board presents Mrs. Reagan with a commemorative egg at the White House on March 25, 1988.

OPPOSITE: Wool dress and matching long jacket with suede belt, designed by Bill Blass.

**SUMMER CELEBRATIONS**    This creamy white linen suit, by Oscar de la Renta, is typical of the style Nancy Reagan favored for official daytime summer events. In July 1986, she packed several crisp white suits for her New York trip celebrating the centennial of the Statue of Liberty. Mrs. Reagan had the honor of cutting the ribbon, allowing visitors to once again climb the statue's stairs after a two-year restoration. "America the Beautiful" blared as 250 doves soared overhead. Children raced for the statue, and the first lady joined them at the base to begin their climb to the top. Within moments Mrs. Reagan appeared, waving out of Liberty's crown. She also presided over the opening of the Ellis Island Immigration Museum. Later, the president reflected, "This was one of the grandest occasions I attended while I was president. What an uplifting experience, unveiling the spruced-up lady and relighting her torch."

LEFT: Two-piece linen suit and leather belt, designed by Oscar de la Renta.

TOP RIGHT: Mrs. Reagan cuts the ceremonial ribbon on Ellis Island on July 5, 1986.

BOTTOM RIGHT: The Reagans on board the USS *Iowa* in New York Harbor on Independence Day, 1986.

OPPOSITE: Mrs. Reagan waves from the crown of the restored Lady Liberty.

President and Mrs. Reagan in the Rose Garden at the 1982 Christmas Tree Lighting ceremony.

OPPOSITE: Wool coat with sash belt, designed by James Galanos.

**CHRISTMAS AT THE WHITE HOUSE**  Mrs. Reagan first wore this green Galanos coat to the Iran hostage release ceremony, shortly after becoming first lady. However, by December, the coat became synonymous with Christmas. She wore it every year to the presentation of the White House Christmas Tree and to the annual White House Tree Lighting ceremony, during which the Reagans ushered the holiday spirit into the nation's capital.

Of course, Christmastime was also a perfect opportunity for Nancy Reagan to don her favorite color, "Reagan Red," and she did so often. In all, she hosted almost a dozen Christmas parties each season. She ensured entertainment and holiday cheer throughout the White House and on the set of "Christmas in Washington," a television broadcast that she and the president hosted annually, starting in 1982.

ABOVE LEFT: The first lady receives the 1983 White House Christmas tree, a twenty-foot noble fir from Washington State.

ABOVE RIGHT: Mrs. Reagan watches the California Raisins perform in the East Room at the White House Christmas party for the children of the diplomatic corps on December 13, 1988.

RIGHT: A boy's choir performs holiday carols at the 1981 White House staff Christmas party.

OPPOSITE: Nancy Reagan decorates the White House Christmas tree in the Blue Room on December 10, 1982.

*These rooms have been filled not only with evergreens and poinsettias, but with families in a festive Christmas spirit. Tonight we are receiving an early present; for here in the East Room we are going to hear voices that sparkle as brilliantly as the lights on these trees.*

— NANCY REAGAN, DECEMBER 20, 1981

# AMERICAN SPLENDOR
## HOSTESS AND AMBASSADOR

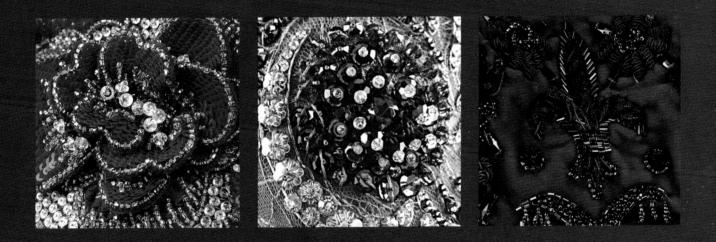

# ENTERTAINING AT THE WHITE HOUSE

*Boy, you can really get a lot accomplished at a state dinner.*

— NANCY REAGAN

One of the first things the wife of an American president learns is that the White House dinner is an integral part of her diplomatic responsibility.

Nancy Reagan looked forward to the challenge, knowing of her husband's desire to reach out to world leaders. By the end of February 1981, the first of many historic dinners was held. "There are dinners which take place almost every month," she recalled. "During our eight years in Washington, Ronnie and I hosted almost eighty of them," which is a staggering number when one understands the complexity of such a feat. Despite the fact that each dinner required several months of planning, to say nothing of addressing hundreds of checklist items, Nancy Reagan did it well and enjoyed it. As she said to CNN's Larry King, "I loved giving the state dinners. I just loved it. How else could you ever give a party like that, Larry?"

During the first term, she spent roughly 450 hours planning more than thirty state dinners. According to *Time* magazine, "She presided at nearly as many other official dinners as well as an additional 250 official White House functions, the picture-perfect but surely enervating flurry of luncheons, teas, receptions. Such occasions require a deep well of small talk and unwavering poise." She tasted and approved virtually every item on every menu.

Imagine. By February 26, 1981, after being in office only thirty-five days, the new administration's first state dinner was held in honor of the United Kingdom's Prime Minister Margaret Thatcher accompanied by her husband, Denis Thatcher.

Several weeks later, Japan's Prime Minister and Mrs. Zenko Suzuki arrived on the South Lawn of the White House for a diplomatic summit. After their meetings, indications were that the leaders were becoming good friends. So, Prime Minister Suzuki offered a toast with a smile, "I would like to mention one more reason why I feel as if President Reagan is an old friend. We were born in the same year and are both proud of being a youthful seventy. I have to admit, however, Mr. President, that I cannot match your health and vitality. This is because I was born, unfortunately, twenty-six days before you, which gives you that much edge."

A vivid illustration of what can be accomplished through a state dinner occurred in June 1986 when the White House welcomed Julio Maria Sanguinetti, president of Uruguay. To the dinner, the Reagans invited many guests who were an

OPPOSITE: Mrs. Reagan escorts the Prince and Princess of Wales down the Central Hall during the dinner in their honor on November 9, 1985. PAGE 94: The Reagans emerge from the Diplomatic Entrance, while "Hail to the Chief" is trumpeted from the balcony above, in the customary White House arrival ceremony reserved for heads of state.

important part of the plan for working with South American leaders. Earlier in the day, the Uruguayan president said, "Mr. President, you have before you today not only the chief of the Executive Branch but also the president of the Supreme Court of Justice, the president of the House of Representatives, who represents the main opposition party, and my party's leader in the Senate, who happens to be the son of the last Uruguayan president to visit here, thirty-one years ago. This environment of harmonious cordiality among the different branches of government and democratic parties is the best evidence we can offer the world of what we have achieved in such a short time."

Appropriately, President and Mrs. Reagan held their last state dinner in honor of Margaret Thatcher in November 1988. Out of gratitude, Prime Minister Thatcher said to the President and Mrs. Reagan, "The nature of mankind is such that the struggle for freedom can never be over. But it's a tribute and a testament to your presidency that, as you leave office and make your way westward, back to California, we know that you have brought to fulfillment the famous prophesy of an English poet: 'And not by eastern windows only, when daylight comes, comes in the light; in front the sun climbs slow, how slowly. But westward, look. The land is bright.'"

DINNER

*Supreme of Pompano in Champagne*
*Fleurons*

*Roast Rack of Lamb Persillees*
*Fresh Mint Sauce*
*Vegetables Printanière*

*Hearts of Romaine Lettuce*
*Brie Cheese*

*Grand Marnier Soufflé*

*Beaulieu Vineyard Pinot Chardonnay*
*Inglenook Cabernet Sauvignon 1974*
*Schramsberg Blanc de Noirs*

THE WHITE HOUSE
*Thursday, February 26, 1981*

LEFT: The menu from the first official state dinner held during the Reagan Administration, honoring Prime Minister Margaret and Denis Thatcher.
RIGHT: Mrs. Reagan admires the chef's specialties, including asparagus and crab mousse and saddle of lamb farcie, prepared for a private dinner on May 2, 1981, for the Prince of Wales.
OPPOSITE: The Blue Room is set for an intimate state visit with President Chadli Bendjedid of Algeria on April 17, 1985.

TOP: A place is set for the president using the Lyndon Johnson china
at the May 7, 1981, state dinner for Prime Minister and Mrs. Zenko Suzuki of Japan.
BOTTOM: President Mubarak of Egypt engages Mrs. Reagan in
conversation at the state dinner held in his honor on January 28, 1988.
OPPOSITE: The State Dining Room is set using the Reagan china for the
White House dinner honoring the Prince and Princess of Wales on November 9, 1985.

*Every first lady makes her own choices, and mine was to become
very involved in planning White House events, right down to the
details: the menu, table settings, flowers, and entertainment.*

— NANCY REAGAN

The first lady listens to the president toast Chancellor and Mrs. Helmut Schmidt
of Germany at the state dinner held in their honor on May 21, 1981.
OPPOSITE: Mrs. Reagan selected this floral arrangement for the June 17, 1986,
state dinner for President and Mrs. Julio Maria Sanguinetti of Uruguay.

Wool day dress with pockets and matching overcoat, designed by Geoffrey Beene.

OPPOSITE: Mrs. Reagan and Madame Bernadette Chirac enjoy tea in the Green Room.

**TEA TIME** Teas and coffees were an important part of Mrs. Reagan's role as first lady, and she held more than eighty of them. Typically, teas were scheduled to follow the arrival ceremony—a finely orchestrated show of pageantry on the South Lawn reserved for heads of state, which showcased the honor guard and the U.S. Marine Band. Teas afforded the first lady an opportunity to speak intimately with the spouses of state leaders. On the afternoon of March 31, 1987, Mrs. Reagan shared tea with Madame Bernadette Chirac, the wife of Jacques Chirac, the president of France. She wore this tailored knit day dress by Geoffrey Beene for the occasion.

Chiffon evening gown with cowl neck, dolman sleeves, and elaborately sequined belt, designed by Valentino.

ABOVE: Sequined rose detail of the belt.

**THEIR IMPERIAL HIGHNESSES OF JAPAN**    As the strains performed by renowned cellist Yo-Yo Ma lingered in the Yellow Oval Room, President and Mrs. Reagan shared parting wishes with their honored guests. The date was October 6, 1987, and the Reagans had just hosted dinner in the Private Dining Room for Their Imperial Highnesses Crown Prince Akihito and Crown Princess Michiko of Japan. It was an intimate evening, with only a few dozen guests present. Wearing this shapely Valentino gown, Mrs. Reagan was an exquisite complement to the princess.

*I think red is the most beautiful color for a lady in the evening.*

— VALENTINO GARAVANI, 2007

Mrs. Reagan and Crown Princess Michiko share tea after dinner in the Private Dining Room.

LEFT: Drawing by Galanos with handwritten notes, which read: (lower left) "White satin tie bow shoe"; (upper right) "earrings," "pearl," and "necklace."

RIGHT: Crepe skirt and chiffon bodice with dolman sleeves and cummerbund detail, designed by James Galanos.

OPPOSITE: President and Mrs. Reagan are poised to greet Prime Minister and Mrs. Ingvar Carlsson for the first Swedish state dinner at the White House in more than twenty years.

**THE PRIME MINISTER OF SWEDEN** On September 9, 1987, as Swedish Prime Minister Ingvar Carlsson and his wife emerged from a black limousine at the North Portico, President and Mrs. Reagan greeted them with warm smiles and handshakes. They escorted their guests of honor up the brilliant white steps. It had been many years since a Swedish Prime Minister had visited the White House, and that night the two countries would toast to their friendship.

Nancy Reagan's striking orange gown was a remarkable choice, marking the only time she wore orange to a state dinner. It exemplifies her love of color, as well as her faith in James Galanos's dramatic design sense. Mr. Galanos always recommended shoes, which were often made by David Evans, to wear with his dresses. On the sketch for this gown he had even drawn the shoe.

**THE SULTAN OF OMAN**   The state dinner for Sultan Qaboos bin Said of Oman was held on April 12, 1983. While a Navy harpist and flutist played for dinner guests as they arrived through the East Wing Entrance, President and Mrs. Reagan escorted His Majesty into the Yellow Oval Room to enjoy private cocktails. This room was also where the Private Residence Guest Book was kept, and the first lady made sure each guest of honor signed it. Yet, in spite of all the effort that Nancy Reagan put into choreographing the evening, she could not foresee the surprise that awaited her. At dinner that night, His Majesty was seated in the customary place of honor on her right, affording him the opportunity to present her with a gift of $300,000 for the National Symphony Orchestra for a chair endowment in her honor.

Dressed in this graceful Galanos sheath, Nancy Reagan struck a simple, refined silhouette. She wore this stately gown again in 1983 to a private White House dinner for Princess Margaret, and then again for a *Vanity Fair* photo shoot in 1995. It is also the gown she chose to wear for her official White House portrait.

Nancy Reagan welcomes Sultan Qaboos bin Said of Oman to the White House.

OPPOSITE: Crepe evening gown with raglan sleeves and modified bustle detail, designed by James Galanos.

**THE PRESIDENT OF URUGUAY**  Mrs. Reagan wore this extraordinary Galanos gown to the state dinner on June 17, 1986, which honored President and Mrs. Julio Maria Sanguinetti of Uruguay. For this dinner, guests were seated in the State Dining Room, which was decorated with centerpieces of peach peonies. They enjoyed a first course of delicate crab, lobster, and cucumber mousse with bow-tie cheese twists. The main course featured tender medallions and quenelles of veal *vol-au-vent* with fennel sauce, romaine leaves filled with June peas, and a spinach and endive salad, complemented by California wines. The U.S. Army Strolling Strings serenaded guests as dessert was served. Following the elegant meal, Presidents Reagan and Sanguinetti shared toasts of appreciation.

In the State Dining Room, President Julio Maria Sanguinetti of Uruguay toasts the president and first lady.

OPPOSITE LEFT: Silk evening gown with beaded bodice and silk sash, designed by James Galanos.

OPPOSITE RIGHT: Mrs. Reagan and guests enjoy a dessert of Giandujas mousse with praline sauce, accompanied by the U.S. Army Strolling Strings.

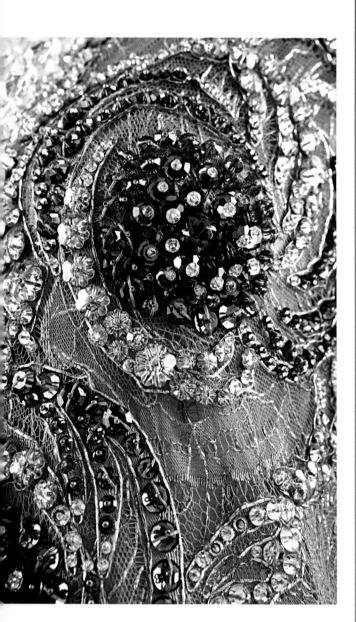

Beaded evening jacket and silk
skirt, designed by James Galanos.

ABOVE: Jacket detail.

After a spirited performance by Julio Iglesias in the East Room, Mrs. Reagan and Mrs. Mitterrand lead guests to the Cross Hall.

**THE PRESIDENT OF FRANCE** The state dinner for His Excellency François Mitterrand, President of France, and his wife, Danielle, was a glittering affair, held on March 22, 1984. Mrs. Reagan hosted the dinner wearing this intricately beaded jacket and silk skirt by Galanos in shades of purple and pink. Among the guests were artists, writers, and personalities, including the photographer Richard Avedon, the designer James Galanos, the decorator Ted Graber, the entertainer Ann-Margret, the singer Julio Iglesias, the actor Jimmy Stewart, and the authors Elie Wiesel, William Styron, and Louis L'Amour. Nancy Reagan thoughtfully created the guest lists and seating arrangements for all of the state dinners, and she took special care with this one, too. She invited distinguished individuals with ties to France whom she thought the Mitterrands would enjoy, such as the actress Olivia de Havilland, the chef Julia Child, and the Parisian artist Marion Pike.

**THE PRIME MINISTER OF THE UNITED KINGDOM**   The first state dinner
the Reagans held, on February 26, 1981, honored the United Kingdom's Prime
Minister Margaret Thatcher and her husband, Denis. The entertainment that
Mrs. Reagan arranged for the night was the celebrated Dance Theatre of Harlem.
Set against the backdrop of the East Room, the choreography of George
Balanchine's *Allegro Brilliante* exuded new life and energy into the White House.
Following the performance, guests moved to the Cross Hall for dancing, while
"The President's Own," the U.S. Marine Band, played, but by that hour the
guests of honor were departing the White House.

Nancy Reagan wrote that she had acquired this delightful gown by James
Galanos sixteen years before entering the White House. While she still loved the
dress, she discussed with the designer freshening it up a little for the first state dinner.
So, Mr. Galanos added two satin straps to each shoulder and tied them in bows.

The president and first lady with
their first state dinner guests, Prime
Minister Margaret Thatcher and
Denis Thatcher, in the Cross Hall.

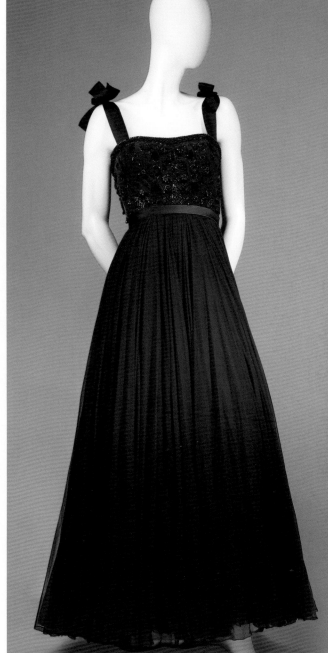

Detail of the bodice.

Tulle evening gown with
embroidered and beaded velvet
bodice, designed by James Galanos.

TOP: President and Mrs. Reagan enjoy a moment with the legendary entertainer Bob Hope in the Cross Hall.

BOTTOM: In the East Room, the Reagans thank the Dance Theatre of Harlem for their performance.

Under the North Portico, the
president and first lady watch as
their guests of honor depart.

# GREETING FRIENDS AND VISITORS

*Mrs. Reagan knew the essentials of a great party were great lighting, great flowers, great food, and a great mix of guests, which produced great distinction and great American style and glamour.*

— CAROLINA HERRERA, 2007

ABOVE LEFT: Mrs. Reagan catches up with actress Elizabeth Taylor at the state dinner for President Li Xiannian of China on July 23, 1985.

ABOVE RIGHT: Tony Randall, who had performed at the White House Special Arts Festival a month earlier, is a special guest at the state dinner held June 18, 1984, for President Jayewardene of Sri Lanka.

RIGHT: At the December 6, 1981, Kennedy Center Honors, the first lady greets Meryl Streep, nominated for that year's Oscar for Best Actress for her role in *The French Lieutenant's Woman.*

OPPOSITE: John Travolta dances with Princess Diana in the Cross Hall to "You're the One that I Want," from the movie *Grease,* at the 1985 White House dinner for the Prince and Princess of Wales.

TOP: Mrs. Reagan presents Jimmy Stewart with a Lifetime Achievement Award at the American Museum for the Moving Image, in New York, on February 25, 1988.

BOTTOM: Cary Grant and Mrs. Reagan share a moment at the private dinner held at the White House for the royal family of Monaco on October 14, 1986.

TOP: Mrs. Reagan speaks with Oscar de la Renta at the 1987 Council of Fashion Designers of America Awards Dinner, after she presented Brooke Astor with a Lifetime Achievement Award.

BOTTOM: Mrs. Reagan welcomes Henry Winkler, who just concluded ten years as "The Fonz" on the sitcom "Happy Days," at the state dinner honoring the Grand Duke and Grand Duchess of Luxembourg on November 13, 1984.

TOP: Mrs. Reagan converses with
Reinaldo and Carolina Herrera in
the Yellow Oval Room at a private
dinner held on October 1, 1983,
for Princess Margaret.

BOTTOM: Karl Lagerfeld and Mrs.
Reagan during the December 4,
1984, state dinner for President
Jaime Lusinchi of Venezuela.

TOP: Mrs. Reagan and Bill Blass
visit in the Private Residence on
May 23, 1988.

BOTTOM: James Galanos dances
with Mrs. Reagan at the state
dinner held for the Mitterrands
on March 22, 1984.

TOP: On October 30, 1985, Mrs. Reagan poses for a photograph with Cher, while Bruce Jenner and Tom Cruise wait their turns.

BOTTOM LEFT: The first lady chats with Warren Beatty and Diane Keaton during a White House screening of the movie *Reds* in December 1981.

BOTTOM RIGHT: Helen Hayes and Mrs. Reagan share tea in the Yellow Oval Room on October 20, 1981.

*We have never had a presidential couple like the two of you. . . . The love and devotion you show to each other isn't seen much around here these days.*

— DANIEL BOORSTIN, LIBRARIAN OF CONGRESS

ABOVE: The Reagans share a dance in the Cross Hall during a state dinner for Chancellor Helmut Schmidt of the Federal Republic of Germany on May 21, 1981.

TOP LEFT: President and Mrs. Reagan with the legendary comedian George Burns at Bob Hope's eightieth birthday tribute at the Kennedy Center on May 20, 1983.

MIDDLE LEFT: Rock Hudson with President and Mrs. Reagan at the May 15, 1984, White House state dinner for President Miguel de la Madrid Hurtado of Mexico.

BOTTOM LEFT: Dinah Shore, Burt Reynolds, and the first lady in the Blue Room during the state visit of Premier Zhao Ziyang of China on January 10, 1984.

# SUPPORTING THE ARTS

*What but art can cause tears among strangers.*

— NANCY REAGAN, 1982

On the South Lawn in July 1981, President and Mrs. Reagan saluted youth in the arts by holding a Mostly Mozart Music Festival and recognizing seventeen-year-old Amanda McKerrow, from Rockville, Maryland, who had won the gold medal at the Moscow International Ballet Competition. This event signaled the birth of Nancy Reagan's "Young Artists in Performance at the White House" program. Quoting Henry James, she said, "It is art that makes life, makes interest, makes importance . . . and I know of no substitute whatever for the force and beauty of its process."

No one understood the importance of the arts in our country and in our culture more than Ronald and Nancy Reagan. As former actors, they embraced the idea from personal experience. As a woman of enormous style, Nancy Reagan conveyed a fashion aesthetic that was an outward symbol of her respect for design. Their combined interests translated into a model for supporting the arts, beginning in Sacramento when they frequently traveled to San Francisco for San Francisco Opera charity events.

The quintessential Reagan political model also applied to their approach to the arts. Basically, they agreed that funding charities is most effectively accomplished by tapping into the resources of the private sector, not into the federal government's public funds.

Once in Washington, bringing attention to the arts was a twofold effort. First of all, their presence at charity events for the arts ensured success for the organization. Secondly, the invitations extended to hundreds of distinguished artists to perform at the White House garnered not only critical attention but exceptional publicity. So organizations like Ford's Theatre, the Kennedy Center, the Joffrey Ballet, the Dance Theatre of Harlem, the Metropolitan Opera, the Phillips Collection, and the Metropolitan Museum of Art, as well as hundreds of individual artists were appreciative recipients of their executive recognition.

To further show their support, President and Mrs. Reagan established the President's Committee on the Arts and the Humanities in 1981. "The arts and humanities have always been something of great personal importance to Nancy and to me," the President declared. "Nations are more often than not remembered for

Mrs. Reagan conducts the orchestra for Maestro Mstislav Rostropovich's sixtieth birthday celebration on March 27, 1987 at the John F. Kennedy Center.

TOP: Isaac Stern performs in the East Room at the
state dinner for Premier Zhao Ziyang of China on January 10, 1984.
BOTTOM: Marvin Hamlisch, Mrs. Reagan, Vic Damone, Bobby Short, and Liza Minnelli,
as the master of ceremonies, rehearse in the East Room on March 8, 1987, for the upcoming
PBS broadcast of "In Performance at the White House, A Tribute to American Music."

their art and thought." The President and Mrs. Reagan believed our cultural institutions are an essential national resource, and they must be kept strong.

A particularly memorable moment in Nancy Reagan's life as first lady took place when the Kennedy Center honored the sixtieth birthday of the cellist Mstislav Rostropovich. At the very end of a concert in which many brilliant musicians participated, Nancy Reagan stole the show by making her debut as a conductor.

The president characterized the Reagans' devotion to the arts when he remarked, "And, as Nancy said earlier, art is no stranger to our national house. Many who lived here have filled it with civilizing beauty. John Fitzgerald Kennedy, who died on this day eighteen years ago, certainly did so. A month before his death, President Kennedy spoke of his vision for American culture. He said, 'I look forward to an America which will not be afraid of grace and beauty . . . which commands respect not only for its strength but for its civilization as well.'"

The Reagans and their guests of honor applaud the entertainment at the
August 5, 1981, state dinner for President and Mrs. Anwar Sadat of Egypt.
PAGES 130–131: On March 28, 1982, the PBS broadcast of "Young Americans in
Performance at the White House" features the San Francisco Ballet in the East Room.

Cocktail dress with beaded and
fringed detail at the sleeves and
hem, designed by Jean Louis.

OPPOSITE: Nancy Reagan
welcomes guests and introduces
Beverly Sills as the master of
ceremonies for the first "Young
Americans in Performance
at the White House."

*I believe art binds us to one another. . . . When we hear an especially touching strain of music or watch a lovely pas de deux, the emotions of an entire audience meld together, and we are one with the performance.*

— NANCY REAGAN,
SEPTEMBER 21, 1982

**IN PERFORMANCE AT THE WHITE HOUSE**  Opening the White House to 100 guests and PBS, Nancy Reagan declared, "Now the East Room becomes a concert hall for the whole nation." On November 22, 1981, she presided over the very first "Young Americans In Performance at the White House," wearing this black cocktail dress with beaded trim. It was an innovative forum that showcased accomplished performers and talented young artists. Beverly Sills, as master of ceremonies, introduced the pianist Rudolph Serkin and the protégé violinist Ida Levin, who opened with Beethoven's "Moonlight" sonata. The *Washington Post* hailed the event as an indisputable "triumph!"

Nancy Reagan's timeless cocktail dress was designed by Jean Louis, the former chief designer for Columbia Pictures. Jean Louis was known for the infamous sequined gown in which Marilyn Monroe serenaded President Kennedy and the iconic black strapless gown Rita Hayworth wore in *Gilda*. Elements of both gowns are recalled in this sophisticated dress.

**FORD'S THEATRE**   On March 21, 1981, at the White House reception that preceded the annual Ford's Theatre benefit performance, politicians and businessmen were excited to brush elbows with famous actors and celebrities in the stately setting of the East Room. Mrs. Reagan facilitated introductions in this white sheath embroidered with beaded palm leaves and daisies. The conversation among guests was restrained, however, as President Reagan had recently announced cutbacks to federal funding of the arts, and the artistic community was having a hard time believing in this politician who had once been one of them. At the time, they could not foresee how tremendous the growth of corporate sponsorship would become under the Reagans' leadership. In 1987, Ford's Theatre recognized this contribution by honoring Nancy Reagan for her years of support. However, the most exciting thrill of that evening came when Mikhail Baryshnikov swirled her around the stage while Sammy Cahn sang, "I've got a case on Nancy with the smiling face."

Nancy Reagan congratulates the evening's performers at the annual Ford's Theatre benefit gala.

Beaded sheath with daisy and palm leaf design.

ABOVE: Detail.

Two-piece beaded evening gown with dolman sleeves, designed by James Galanos.

ABOVE: Detail of the beaded neckline.

The Reagans welcome the Kennedy Center honorees Virgil Thomson, Elia Kazan, Frank Sinatra, Katherine Dunham, and Jimmy Stewart in the East Room.

**THE KENNEDY CENTER HONORS**   Every year, President and Mrs. Reagan joyfully shared in the Kennedy Center's tribute to five Americans who "contributed significantly to American culture through the performing arts." Nancy Reagan wore this elaborately beaded gown by Galanos to the December 4, 1983, gala and White House reception. That year, two special friends from the Reagans' Hollywood days were being celebrated, Jimmy Stewart and Frank Sinatra, along with honorees Elia Kazan, Virgil Thomson, and Katherine Dunham. The Kennedy Center Honors were always a high point for the president and the first lady. Mrs. Reagan fondly recalled the 1988 event, when their support was appreciated in grand style. Walter Cronkite came out on stage and remarked, "For eight years, two people have sat up there in that box alongside our honorees. The years have gone swiftly by, but, President and Mrs. Reagan, we'd like to detain you long enough to say thank you." And on that note, the entire Kennedy Center crew lined the stage and began to sing "Auld Lang Syne." Mrs. Reagan reminisced, "That's a song that does me in under any circumstance. And, of course, I started to cry."

**ON STAGE AT THE MET** The Metropolitan Opera in New York City held its annual benefit dinner entitled "On Stage at the Met" on March 22, 1987. Wearing this luxuriant velvet Carolina Herrera gown, Nancy Reagan was the star of the gala. As she arrived at the opera, the press began asking her political questions that were irrelevant to the event, so, according to Ms. Herrera, Mrs. Reagan turned it "into a fashion moment with her fantastic response, 'This is Carolina Herrera,' as she walked into the opera." And, upon entry, Nancy Reagan received a standing ovation. That night she was being recognized by the opera for her leadership role in promoting corporate sponsorship of the arts, which had not been widely embraced before Reagan's presidency. She was the first nonmember of the Metropolitan Opera to be honored with this distinction.

Mrs. Reagan wore this elegant gown again for the state dinner held in honor of President Mubarak of Egypt on January 28, 1988.

*Nancy Reagan has such a great sense of fashion and style that her look is timeless.*

— CAROLINA HERRERA, 2007

On stage with Cecile Zilkha, Mrs. Reagan accepts honors bestowed by the Metropolitan Opera in New York City.

Velvet evening gown with
knotted sash in back, designed
by Carolina Herrera.

Silk evening gown with
three-quarter sleeves, silk sash,
and sequined skirt, designed
by Valentino.

*[Princess Grace's] friendship will stay with me always —*
*I will long remember our days in Hollywood together.*

— NANCY REAGAN, OCTOBER 15, 1986

Michael Feinstein, after playing a few American standards for the royal family of Monaco, jokes with the president and first lady.

**HONORING HER SERENE HIGHNESS**   Nancy Reagan wore this black Valentino gown with a sequined skirt for a private dinner held at the White House in honor of the royal family of Monaco on October 14, 1986. The following day, Nancy Reagan unveiled the sculpted portrait of Her Serene Highness Princess Grace at a ceremony in the National Portrait Gallery. The sculpture was to commemorate the Princess's support of the arts and her untimely passing in September 1982. Mrs. Reagan shared a deep love for the arts with the former fellow MGM star, and the two were friends from their Hollywood days. Like Nancy Reagan at the White House, Princess Grace frequently used her position in the Royal Palace to showcase and support the arts. In March 1983, Mrs. Reagan had honored her friend by performing a twenty-minute reading of "Carnival of the Animals," at a benefit for the National Symphony Orchestra. It was a poem that Princess Grace had been planning to read at the event. "Having never done anything like that before, I was terrified," recalled Mrs. Reagan. "It wasn't just a reading—it was set to the music of the symphony." Nonetheless, it garnered her a standing ovation.

# THE BRITISH RELATIONSHIP

*It is only nine months since we had the great pleasure of having you and Mrs. Reagan stay with us at Windsor. Now, we have had the memorable experience of visiting you in your home State of California and of seeing your ranch at Santa Barbara. I knew before we came that we had exported many of our traditions to the United States. But I had not realized before that weather was one of them. But, Mr. President, if the climate has been cool, your welcome and that of the American people have been wonderfully warm.*

— HER ROYAL MAJESTY QUEEN ELIZABETH II, MARCH 1983

For the Reagans, relations with those "across the pond" began years before life at 1600 Pennsylvania Avenue. Nancy Reagan remembers when they "met Charles in Palm Springs when Ronnie was governor." Then, in March 1975, the Reagans met Margaret Thatcher. "I liked her immediately," Ronald Reagan recalled, "she was warm, feminine, gracious, and intelligent—and it was evident from our first words that we were soul mates when it came to reducing government and expanding economic freedom."

The president and his first lady expressed their immense respect for their British friends in many ways, saving the first and last state dinners to honor Margaret Thatcher. Fortunately, they were graced with the presence of Her Royal Majesty Queen Elizabeth II, at the first dinner in February 1981. In that same year, Nancy Reagan represented America at the royal wedding of Charles and Diana, and then returned in 1982 to listen to her husband address Parliament. At that time, the queen hosted a state dinner in their honor. Nancy Reagan remembered, "Ronnie . . . was seated between Queen Elizabeth and the queen mother. Apparently, 'The Shooting of Dan McGrew' is also a favorite of the queen mother's. I don't remember how it began, but before I knew it the two of them were reciting that poem together—all eleven stanzas—back and forth at the table!"

In 1983, Queen Elizabeth II and Prince Philip not only visited Rancho del Cielo, the Reagans' Santa Barbara ranch, but also invited President and Mrs. Reagan for an anniversary dinner aboard the *Britannia*, the royal yacht. Nancy Reagan remembers her husband saying, "I know I promised Nancy a lot of things thirty-one years ago, but I never promised her *this.*"

President and Mrs. Reagan depart Windsor Castle on June 9, 1982.
The previous day, the president addressed Parliament at the House of Lords, delivering
a fiery speech in support of democracy.

The year 1985 recorded some particularly memorable moments for Nancy Reagan. At a dinner hosted by Margaret Thatcher at the British Embassy in Washington, Lady Thatcher said, in her toast, "We in Britain think you are a wonderful president. And from one old hand to another, welcome to a second term. And Denis will be saying exactly the same to Nancy. And neither of us could have done what we've done without them."

Several months later, in November, the eyes of the world were on Washington when President and Mrs. Reagan hosted the Prince and Princess of Wales. Then Mrs. Reagan was off to Westminster Abbey for the wedding of Prince Andrew and Sarah Ferguson. And, in 1988, the queen extended an invitation for tea at Buckingham Palace to the American first lady.

On two occasions, Nancy and Ronald Reagan hosted Margaret Thatcher at Camp David, the secluded presidential retreat that was their private escape for eight years. Finally, at the welcoming ceremony in November 1988, prior to the final state dinner, a smiling Ronald Reagan with Nancy at his side saluted Margaret Thatcher and said, "Prime Minister Thatcher, here is a story from our Old West. It's said that a cowboy went out riding one day and suddenly stumbled into the Grand Canyon. And he's supposed to have said, 'Wow, something sure has happened here!' Well, Prime Minister Thatcher, when we contemplate the world as it is today and how it was when we first met here eight years ago, we too have a right to say: Something sure has happened."

Mrs. Reagan and Her Majesty Queen Elizabeth II are accompanied by Colonel Gerard Leigh, chairman of the Guards Polo Club, to a polo match at Smith's Lawn in London, July 26, 1981, during the first lady's visit for the royal wedding of the Prince of Wales and Lady Diana Spencer.

Mrs. Reagan is interviewed on the
morning of July 29, 1981.

LEFT: Silk crepe faille blouse, skirt, and shirt-coat embellished with a moiré lapel, and a matching chiffon scarf and hat, all designed by James Galanos.

RIGHT: Mrs. Reagan descends the steps of St. Paul's Cathedral after the Prince and Princess of Wales are wed.

**THE ROYAL WEDDING: THE PRINCE AND PRINCESS OF WALES**    The wedding of Prince Charles and Lady Diana Spencer on July 29, 1981, was one of the most celebrated spectacles of the decade. Requesting something simple but flexible, Mrs. Reagan relied on Mr. Galanos to provide a classic look for the highly publicized event. Seated just six rows from the altar, she wore this soft peach ensemble with a matching shirt-coat. The press, which before the event had been clamoring, to no avail, for a description of her dress, reported that "Nancy Reagan was elegantly turned out." Due to the recent attempt on his life, President Reagan could not attend. He encouraged Mrs. Reagan to serve as the United States representative. She spent one week in London, the longest she had been away from the president in twenty-nine years, and attended eighteen events on behalf of the nation.

Silk printed shirt-coat and
black leather belt, designed by
James Galanos.

Nancy Reagan arrives for a private tour of St. Paul's Cathedral.

**ST PAUL'S CATHEDRAL**   Nancy Reagan first wore this printed silk coat and a matching long-sleeve day dress designed by Galanos in London on July 27, 1981. One of the many appointments scheduled during her busy trip for the royal wedding of Prince Charles and Lady Diana was a visit to St. Paul's Cathedral. Wearing this classic black and white ensemble, she toured the grand cathedral and the American Memorial Chapel. Two days later she would return to St. Paul's Cathedral for the majestic wedding ceremony.

Mrs. Reagan also wore this dress and coat to the Vatican Pontifical Palace in Rome on June 7, 1982, when the president and first lady received a tour through the palace grounds prior to their visit with the pope. Mrs. Reagan then changed out of this outfit and into a more stately dress for her official audience with His Holiness.

*Nancy Reagan is a timeless symbol of American elegance.*

— VALENTINO GARAVANI, 2007

**THE ROYAL WEDDING: THE DUKE AND DUCHESS OF YORK**   In July 1986, Nancy Reagan again served as the official United States representative to a British royal event, the wedding of Prince Andrew and Sarah Ferguson. To the wedding, held on July 23 at Westminster Abbey, she wore a soft aqua silk dress and shirt-coat by Galanos. Its subtle elegance was reminiscent of the peach silk ensemble he designed for the 1982 wedding of Prince Charles and Lady Diana. Two days prior to Prince Andrew's wedding, the first lady wore this two-piece Valentino gown to a private dinner hosted by Major and Mrs. Ronald Ferguson at the Windsor Great Park Polo Grounds. From the delicate embroidery of the bodice, to the turned cuffs with pearl buttons, to the shirring at the hip, this gown embodies the feminine details that are quintessential Valentino.

Beaded chiffon blouse, shirred crepe skirt, and jewel-embellished belt, designed by Valentino.

Mrs. Reagan at Winfield House, residence of the U.S. Ambassador to the Court of St. James, Charles Price, where she stayed during her quick trip to London for the royal wedding of Prince Andrew and Sarah Ferguson.

LEFT: Detail of the blouse.

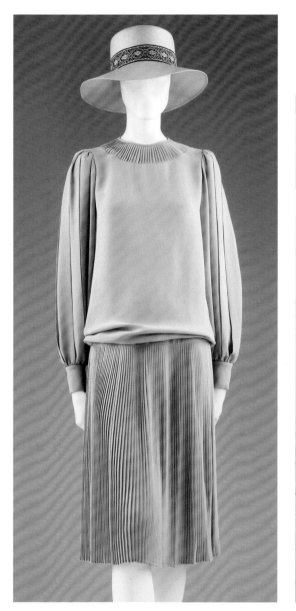

**ARRIVAL AT WINDSOR CASTLE**    Nancy Reagan deplaned Air Force One with the president on June 7, 1982, wearing this understated, yet stylish, silk skirt and blouson top designed by Galanos. In a traditional arrival ceremony, President and Mrs. Reagan were welcomed by Her Majesty Queen Elizabeth II and Prince Philip in the magnificent gardens of Windsor Castle. It was their second trip to the United Kingdom since becoming president and first lady and was just one of the stops on the Reagans' tour of Europe surrounding the economic summit in Versailles.

LEFT: Silk blouson top with pleated sleeves, matching pleated skirt, and straw hat, designed by James Galanos.

RIGHT: Greeted by Prince Philip, President and Mrs. Reagan arrive at Heathrow Airport on Air Force One.

Her Majesty Queen Elizabeth II,
President Reagan, First Lady
Nancy Reagan, and Prince Philip
stroll through the rose garden
at Windsor Castle.

*And when I traveled abroad, I thought I should represent our country in the best possible light.*

— NANCY REAGAN

**FRIENDS AT WINDSOR CASTLE**    On the day President Reagan spoke of his steadfast commitment to democracy in a speech before Parliament, the Reagans attended a spectacular, yet intimate, banquet given by Her Majesty, the Queen of England. At the dinner on June 8, 1982, among other summit leaders and their spouses, President and Mrs. Reagan conveyed confidence, optimism, and charm. They were an enchanting vision of leadership, the first lady in this beaded Galanos gown and the president in his full evening-dress attire. Loyalty was a character trait the Reagans held dear in their personal life, and it was a virtue that the president demonstrated in political spheres as well. In this majestic setting, among other world leaders, President and Mrs. Reagan assured America's friends that they knew the meaning of alliance.

LEFT: Printed and beaded silk evening gown with bateau neck, bishop sleeves, and front slit, designed by James Galanos.

TOP RIGHT: Sleeve detail.

MIDDLE RIGHT: The first lady glances lovingly at her husband.

BOTTOM RIGHT: The Reagans with their hosts at Windsor Castle.

Queen Elizabeth is escorted by
President Reagan and First Lady
Nancy Reagan is escorted by
Prince Philip.

# REPRESENTING AMERICA ABROAD

*America has a lot of friends . . . I come home with a message*
*from our allies. We are not alone. They are with us.*

— RONALD REAGAN, JUNE 11, 1982

Here is a typical itinerary of a trip abroad for an American president and his first lady. It began in June 1982, at . . .

*June 2, The White House South Lawn*: President and Mrs. Reagan were helicoptered to Andrews Air Force Base where Air Force One was ready to escort them to France.

*June 6, Versailles*: While her husband met with six other world leaders for the Versailles Economic Summit, Nancy Reagan flew to Normandy to visit Omaha Beach. As she toured the beach, she paused before a German bunker, preserved as a memorial, with the words of Franklin Roosevelt carved across its top: "We would rather die on our feet than live on our knees."

*June 7, The Vatican*: This memorable visit to see His Holiness Pope John Paul II proved meaningful, yet taxing, as the Reagans were terribly fatigued by jet lag. "I met with him seven times, and twice alone, which was really a wonderful, wonderful experience," said Nancy Reagan, "but, you know, he and Ronnie had so many things in common—they both were actors, avid sportsmen, and both were targets of would-be assassins at approximately the same time." In honor of their visit, a group of American seminarians sang "America the Beautiful" in the Vatican. President Reagan recalled that it was as "lovely a rendition as I had ever heard it. Nancy and I were both in tears." Lunch with the president of Italy followed and then a meeting with the prime minister.

*Air Force One*: For the first time, a "Do Not Disturb" sign was placed on the Reagans' door so they could rest.

*June 7, Windsor Castle*: In an exciting arrival ceremony, Queen Elizabeth welcomed the President and Mrs. Reagan in the magnificent gardens of Windsor Castle. They dined together that evening. Surprisingly, the Reagans were the first American president and first lady to be hosted by the queen at Windsor and the first to spend two nights in the castle.

*June 8, Royal Gallery at the Palace of Westminster*: With both Houses of Parliament and the first lady as his audience, Ronald Reagan delivered a speech with flawless timing and resonance.

President and Mrs. Reagan depart the South Lawn on Marine One for Andrews Air Force Base as they head to the Soviet Union for the Moscow Summit on May 25, 1988.

*June 9, 10 Downing Street*: While President Reagan was meeting with Margaret Thatcher, Nancy Reagan read the London papers, which declared the visit as "tremendously successful" and described her husband as "a wonderful old smoothie."

*June 9, Bonn*: President Reagan delivered a speech to the West German Bundestag, which was one of the major successes of this tour. The speech included his famous "You are not alone" line. Reporters documented how crowds in Bonn were as captivated by the stunning first lady's wardrobe as they were invigorated by her husband's inspiring words. A NATO summit followed on June 10.

*June 11, West Berlin*: The Reagans arrived at Tempelhof Airport, now a U.S. military installation. A little girl slipped between the legs of a Secret Service agent and thrust a bouquet at President Reagan as he was reviewing troops. Without breaking stride, the president grasped the flowers in his left hand while continuing to salute with his right. Quite unintentionally, the incident symbolized the image he was trying to convey to Europe: military determination on the one hand, offers of negotiation and arms control on the other.

After a visit to the Berlin Wall, where for a brief moment he mischievously put one foot over a line marking the no-man's land between the two zones, the president, with the first lady in attendance, pursued what had become a full-fledged peace offensive in a speech at the Charlottenburg Palace.

*June 11, Bonn*: Mrs. Reagan proudly remembers her husband's parting words at the last stop of the trip: "Diplomacy is important, but friendship leaves an even more lasting impression. Your friendship for us has been an especially moving experience."

*June 11, Andrews Air Force Base*: Fifteen thousand well-wishers gathered to welcome President and Mrs. Reagan home. In 10,659 miles of travel through five nations in ten days, and meetings with a pope, a queen, and heads of government of the fifteen other NATO countries, the president and the first lady confirmed that America does indeed have many allies.

President Reagan, in his tuxedo, and Mrs. Reagan, in a one-shouldered evening gown by James Galanos, are the guests of honor at a banquet dinner hosted by President François and Danielle Mitterrand in the Hall of Mirrors at Versailles, France, after the June 1982 economic summit.

*When I knew she was going to be in Europe, I'd say, "Nancy, let's do something a little more interesting," and she would leave it up to me.*

— JAMES GALANOS, 2007

**IN MADRID WITH QUEEN SOFIA** "Nancy with the Flamenco Feet" was how the *Washington Post* hailed it. On May 7, 1985, while in Madrid with the president during his tour of Europe for the 1985 economic summit, Mrs. Reagan began her day viewing a flamenco performance given by Spanish children at the Royal School of Dance and Dramatic Arts. With good humor, she accepted the instructor's invitation to come on stage for few pointers after the show concluded. "Her footwork showed promise" and "her movements were fluid," the press reported. And her host for the day enjoyed it too. "She had great rhythm—fantastic," professed Queen Sofia. Dressed in this Galanos suit with coordinating blouse and scarf, Mrs. Reagan had her first lesson of the crash course in Spanish culture given by the queen of Spain.

Wool suit with coordinating silk blouse and scarf, designed by James Galanos.

**OPPOSITE:** Mrs. Reagan learns to dance the flamenco with the Royal School of Dance and Dramatic Arts in Madrid, Spain.

*We walked into this other room and some American visitors
and a lot of young priests were singing "America the Beautiful."
It brought tears to my eyes, and also my husband's.*

— NANCY REAGAN, 1982

**HIS HOLINESS POPE JOHN PAUL II**    On June 7, 1982, President and Mrs.
Reagan paid their first visit to His Holiness Pope John Paul II, at the Papal Library
of the Vatican. An audience with the pope was a highlight of their trip to Europe,
which had included the economic summit in Versailles. Mrs. Reagan was especially
touched when the seminarians of the North American College in Rome sang
"America the Beautiful." The Reagans were given a second audience with the pope
on June 6, 1987. On both occasions, the first lady dressed in this floor-length
Adolfo ensemble and black lace mantilla, accessorized with opera pearls.

Nancy Reagan treasured her meetings with the pope. She even met with
him alone in 1985 to discuss her anti-drug crusade. On that occasion, which was
more of a business meeting, her dress was much different. She wore a black skirt
suit with white trim and a matching hat.

President and Mrs. Reagan are
greeted by American cardinals in
the Clementine Room of the
Vatican Pontifical Palace during
their 1982 visit with His Holiness
Pope John Paul II.

OPPOSITE: Crepe blouse with
Jabot collar, matching skirt with
ruffled hem, and belt, designed
by Adolfo.

*Mrs. Reagan's approach to fashion, as well as mine, is to create a chic, timeless look that is effective not just today, but tomorrow as well.*

— ADOLFO, 2007

**EXPLORING CHINA** Nancy Reagan spent many hours studying Chinese history and culture in the months before the Reagans' historic trip to China in April and May 1984. The trip began in Beijing, where she visited the Peking Zoo and presented more than $13,000 she had raised as honorary chair of the World Wildlife Fund's "Pennies for Pandas" campaign. Together, President and Mrs. Reagan then traveled outside Beijing, where they marveled at the magnitude of the Great Wall and stood shoulder to shoulder among the soldiers of the Terracotta Army in Xi'an. In addition to seeing China's great monuments, Nancy Reagan was interested in meeting China's citizenry. In Beijing, Xi'an, and Shanghai she toured neighborhood clinics, met with women's groups, and visited schoolchildren. The press noticed that she dressed in her reliably polished and versatile Adolfo suits for many of these visits.

The first lady is greeted by Shanghai kindergarteners at the Rainbow Bridge Township Day Care Center on May 1, 1984.

TOP: Ronald Reagan, the first American president to visit China in twelve years, and his wife admire the Great Wall on April 28, 1984.

Guided by a member of the All
China Women's Federation, Mrs.
Reagan tours the Temple of Heaven
in Beijing on April 27, 1984.

# FORGING RELATIONS WITH RUSSIA

*I am familiar with your Constitution but I wish
your husband could stay on for another four years.*

— MIKHAIL GORBACHEV, MAY 31, 1988

After an important meeting with President Reagan in Washington in 1984, Soviet foreign minister Andrei Gromyko was escorted into the Red Room to be greeted by the first lady. She offered him something to drink, and the foreign minister asked, "Does your husband believe in peace or war?" "Peace," she said. "You're sure?" Yes, she said, she was sure, and the conversation floated back to more effervescent subjects. When it came time for the two men to go in to lunch, Gromyko returned to the issue. "Well, then," he instructed the president's wife, "you whisper *peace* in his ear every night." "I will," she replied. "I'll also whisper it in your ear." Shortly after this meeting, General Secretary Mikhail Gorbachev and President Reagan would finally engage in face-to-face diplomacy. Nancy Reagan observed from the moment the two leaders met that they had a special connection. Seated at dinner in the Kremlin, Gorbachev turned to her and said, "You know, your husband and I have a certain . . . ," and he could not find the right words. "Let me help you," Nancy Reagan replied, "chemistry?"

After four meetings—Geneva, Reykjavik, Washington, and Moscow—Nancy Reagan understood these two world leaders had developed a mutual respect and affection for each other. But getting there was not easy for the first lady.

First ladies serve as symbols of American culture. In Nancy Reagan's first trip to Geneva, she met with Raisa Gorbachev, the general secretary's wife. Interestingly, their clothing became a metaphor for the different ideologies they represented: Nancy Reagan, dressed in warm colors and elegant, classic designs, revealed her personal style while showing respect for the importance of the meeting. In a sense, her clothing symbolized the right to individual expression protected by our Constitution. Conversely, Raisa Gorbachev's outfit—stern, matronly, and essentially, a uniform—was symbolic of socialist ideology, which suppressed personal expression.

Thankfully, the president's objective was met in Geneva. As Nancy Reagan said, "Above all, he had wanted to establish a personal working relationship with Gorbachev. Everything else would follow from that."

After another meeting in Reykjavik, the next summit was held in Washington, where Mrs. Reagan oversaw the planning of a grand state dinner. She had asked

The Reagans greet the Gorbachevs at the Grand Kremlin Palace during
the opening ceremony of the Moscow Summit on May 29, 1988.

pianist Van Cliburn to perform, and everyone in Washington was clamoring for an invitation. Celebrities like Joe DiMaggio, Meadowlark Lemon, Mary Lou Retton, Jimmy Stewart, Pearl Bailey, and Billy Graham were included, to name a few.

The last summit in Moscow required Nancy Reagan to study up on Soviet art and culture, learn a few Russian phrases, and leave the formal evening dress behind. She decided to play it safe and not wear anything red, fearing it might be perceived as inappropriate or offensive.

When in Moscow, she asked Raisa Gorbachev if religious services were held in any of the beautiful cathedrals she saw. The Russian first lady curtly replied, "Nyet." However, Mrs. Reagan was received warmly by the Russian people she met. At a school, a young boy told her, "We hope the gun will never be used again." She was equally touched when four village women greeted her holding lilacs. "We're so happy to see you," they said. "We're so glad you came. We've waited for you for so long. All we want is for our children to live under blue skies—and no war."

President Reagan and General Secretary Mikhail Gorbachev sign
the Intermediate-range Nuclear Forces (INF) Treaty in the East Room of the
White House on December 8, 1987, during the Washington summit.

Mikhail Gorbachev and Nancy Reagan toast at the Soviet Embassy dinner on December 9, 1987.

**MAISON DE SAUSSURE, GENEVA**   Prior to her first tea with Raisa Gorbachev, which took place in Geneva on November 19, 1985, Nancy Reagan anticipated discussing the personal similarities that she and Mrs. Gorbachev shared, such as being in the limelight that came with marriage to a world leader. As it turned out, these two women were far too different, in personality and circumstance, to enjoy such ease at this critical juncture in their countries' relationship. "There was a fire in the fireplace, but the conversation was dry, impersonal," Mrs. Reagan recalled. The first lady dressed in this smart Galanos suit for the tea at Maison de Saussure, which lasted just over an hour.

Later, Nancy Reagan was pleased to discover that conversation with Mikhail Gorbachev was more relaxed, and that he had a fine sense of humor. During the intimate dinner she and President Reagan hosted for the Gorbachevs at Maison de Saussure, General Secretary Gorbachev shared personal stories of his youth and inquired about Hollywood. "From then on, the more I saw him, the more I liked him," Mrs. Reagan wrote.

Nancy Reagan welcomes Raisa Gorbachev to Maison de Saussure during the Geneva summit.

TOP: Blouse detail.

BOTTOM: Drawing by Galanos with handwritten note: "Nancy—Blouse worn over skirt and extends beyond jacket to form border design— again if it doesn't suit you tuck in Blouse normally into skirt."

Wool suit with hounds-tooth jacket and coordinating silk blouse, designed by James Galanos.

*For all my difficulties with Raisa, I knew she was under pressures that I couldn't even imagine, and I didn't envy her.*

— NANCY REAGAN

Tea is served for the first ladies and their interpreters in the drawing room of Maison de Saussure.

OPPOSITE: Nancy Reagan.

Mrs. Reagan and Mrs. Gorbachev are seated for tea at the Soviet Mission to the United Nations during the Geneva summit.

OPPOSITE: Wool tweed suit with coordinating silk blouse, designed by James Galanos.

**TEA AT THE SOVIET MISSION**   The day after their first meeting, it was Raisa Gorbachev's turn to host Nancy Reagan for tea at the Soviet Mission to the United Nations in Geneva. Mrs. Reagan arrived wearing this Galanos gray suit. Raisa Gorbachev, in contrast, was starkly dressed. Nancy Reagan later learned that Mrs. Gorbachev was wearing the standard uniform of Soviet teachers, and that the photographs taken that day would be the only ones shown to the Russian people. Their relationship remained strained until 1988, after the INF Treaty was ratified. Looking back, Nancy Reagan reflected, "If Raisa and I had been left alone, without any press, we probably would have had an easier time of it."

**THE STATE DINNER FOR THE SOVIETS**   On the evening of December 8, 1987, jubilation flowed through the White House. President Reagan and General Secretary Gorbachev had signed the INF Treaty in the East Room earlier that day, and the excitement was far from dwindling. This state dinner was going to be unlike any other. For the evening's entertainment, Mrs. Reagan had asked pianist Van Cliburn to perform, and, although Mr. Cliburn had not played in public in nine years, he obliged the first lady. She had sought him out specifically because he was a favorite among Russians ever since he won the Tchaikovsky Piano Competition in Moscow in 1958. Having had only a few weeks to put together what usually takes months, Mrs. Reagan must have felt satisfaction as the General Secretary thanked Mr. Cliburn for his performance with a big bear hug. The first lady wore this black and pink gown with Galanos's signature beadwork for the stately affair.

This spectacular event followed a very difficult two months in Nancy Reagan's personal life, in which she had battled breast cancer and suffered the loss of her mother. Reflecting upon this time, Bernard Shaw of CNN remarked, "She did it all with grace and dignity."

The Reagans and Gorbachevs celebrate the signing of the INF Treaty in the Red Room, prior to the state dinner honoring the general secretary and his wife on December 8, 1987.

Beaded evening gown with
openwork sleeves and satin bow
sash, designed by James Galanos.

ABOVE: Sleeve detail.

**THE DANILOV MONASTERY**    Six months after the INF Treaty signing at the White House, it was President and Mrs. Reagan's turn to travel to the Soviet Union to exchange the ratified treaties. The trip, from May 29 to June 2, 1988, was in many ways a cultural expedition. The president had been urging Soviet leaders to grant more religious freedom, and on May 30 the Reagans met with eighteen Russian Orthodox monks from the Danilov Monastery. Built in the late thirteenth century, it is the home of the patriarch of the Russian Orthodox Church and Russia's oldest Orthodox monastery. However, after the 1917 Bolshevik Revolution, the monastery had been used as a bike factory and then a prison. It was finally returned to the monks in 1983. At the end of the Reagans' visit, the monks were enamored of America's first lady, who wore this graceful day dress by Oscar de la Renta, and presented her with a bouquet of red roses.

Linen day dress with cape sleeves and wide belt, designed by Oscar de la Renta.

**OPPOSITE:** The Danilov monks show their appreciation for the Reagans' promotion of religious freedom in the Soviet Union by presenting the first lady with a bouquet of roses.

*During eight years of White House life, I heard our anthem played hundreds, if not thousands, of times. But never did it sound as grand and imposing as it did that night, in that breathtaking setting.*

— NANCY REAGAN

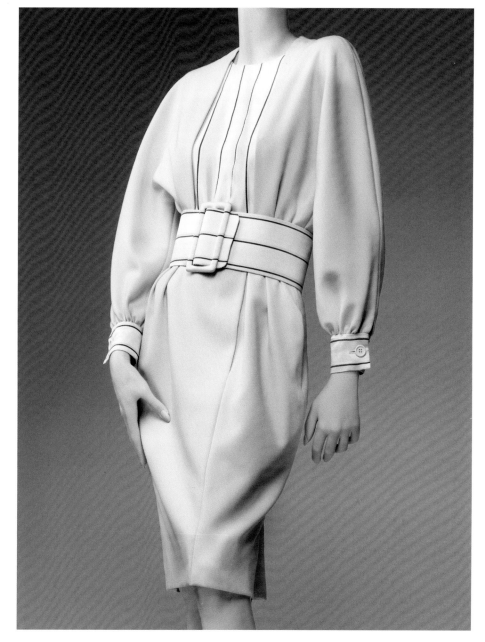

Wool day dress with satin placket, cuffs, and wide belt, designed by James Galanos.

OPPOSITE: The Reagans delight in the colorful domes of St. Basil's Cathedral in Red Square on the last night of the Moscow summit.

**THE BOLSHOI BALLET**    On their last evening in Moscow, June 1, 1988, the president and Mrs. Reagan, attired in this short, white dress by Galanos, joined the Gorbachevs in the royal box of the Bolshoi Theater. "The royal box was flanked by American and Soviet flags," Nancy Reagan remembered, "and as the four of us stood together while the orchestra played our two national anthems, I was just overwhelmed by the pageantry of it all." The ninety-minute ballet included excerpts from *Sleeping Beauty, Romeo and Juliet,* and *Swan Lake.* A relaxing dinner followed at the Gorbachevs' country home, and it was close to midnight when the exhausted couple drove through Red Square. It had already been a memorable night, but President Reagan wanted his wife to see the square, so they got out of the car and strolled, admiring the illuminated onion domes of St. Basil's Cathedral.

The Reagans are welcomed home
at Andrews Air Force Base on
June 3, 1988, after the INF Treaty
is ratified by both nations.

**A NEW ERA IN HISTORY**   Returning to Andrews Air Force Base, the president and Mrs. Reagan, in this very chic ensemble by Oscar de la Renta, stepped off Air Force One to the ringing of a twenty-one-gun salute, blaring trumpets, and cheers from thousands of onlookers. The date was June 3, 1988, and the president had exchanged instruments of ratification of the INF Treaty with Mikhail Gorbachev in Moscow, making the treaty official. America's friendship with Moscow was indeed evidenced by this historical event. Signifying the depth of this friendship, President Reagan, in his farewell remarks to Gorbachev the day before, declared: "Tell the people of the Soviet Union of the deep feelings of friendship felt by us and by the people of our country toward them. Tell them too, Nancy and I are grateful for their coming out to see us, grateful for their waves and smiles, and tell them we will remember all of our days their faces: the faces of hope—hope for a new era in human history."

OPPOSITE: Wool suit and cashmere sweater with gathered shoulder detail and belt, designed by Oscar de la Renta.

TOP: Detail of leather belt and button.

BOTTOM: President Reagan and General Secretary Gorbachev sign the ratified INF Treaty in St. Vladimir's Hall at the Grand Kremlin Palace on June 1, 1988.

# PUBLIC SERVANT
# AND SPOKESWOMAN

# PROMOTING FOSTER GRANDPARENTS

*You can't be pessimistic about anything. You always have
to be optimistic that you can solve something, anything, in life.*

— NANCY REAGAN

There is a grand tradition of first ladies adopting causes. Eleanor Roosevelt was dedicated to the cause of human welfare, Bess Truman adopted the Muscular Dystrophy Association, and Lady Bird Johnson fostered America's beautification.

Like her predecessors, Nancy Reagan embraced several causes, and these had captured her heart before moving to Washington. While first lady of California, she made regular visits to hospitals and homes for the elderly, as well as schools for physically and emotionally handicapped children. During one of these hospital visits in 1967, she observed participants in the Foster Grandparent program, a program that brings together senior citizens and children, and she soon became its champion.

As first lady of the United States, Mrs. Reagan helped expand the program on a national level and promoted private funding in local communities. It was one of the many commitments on her busy agenda. "Let me say on behalf of Nancy, who couldn't be here but who wanted to," said President Reagan at a White House reception, "she's got a schedule too, I found out. I used to just come home and open the front door and say, 'I'm home.' And now I come home, look through 132 rooms, and then look at her schedule to know where she is."

With Jane Wilkie, she coauthored a book, *To Love a Child*, and a song by the same title was written and dedicated to her by Hal David and Joe Raposo. Frank Sinatra recorded the song, and all proceeds from the book and record sales have gone to the Foster Grandparents program.

As a measure of the power of a first lady's attention, in the program's first year of operation, 782 foster grandparents carried out thirty-three projects in twenty-seven states. By 1985, some 19,000 foster grandparents served some 65,000 children through 245 projects in all fifty states, Puerto Rico, the Virgin Islands, and the District of Columbia.

"She got on an airplane and hardly ever came back to the White House," remembers Sheila Tate, her press secretary. "She was on the road month after month. . . . She invited the press to come with her. She took the camera that you were shining on her and turned it around and focused it on a cause—one she could do something about."

OPPOSITE: Mrs. Reagan garners support for the Foster Grandparents program
from Mickey Mouse at Walt Disney World's Epcot Center on June 9, 1988.
PAGE 186: On July 21, 1981, while in London for the royal wedding of Prince Charles and
Lady Diana, Mrs. Reagan makes time to visit a child with special needs at the Spastics Society.

*It's one of the best programs I've ever seen because it benefits both sides: children, who need love, and grandparents, elderly people, who need to feel wanted.*

— NANCY REAGAN

**THE FIRST FOSTER GRANDPARENTS CONFERENCE**  More than 150 supporters of the Foster Grandparents program came out for its first conference, held in Somersworth, New Hampshire, on October 16, 1987. Wearing this polished Oscar de la Renta tweed suit, the first lady arrived at Maplewood Elementary School ready to guide the program's new initiative. As a direct result of Mrs. Reagan's dedication to this program and to anti-drug awareness, Foster Grandparents had just announced a nationwide effort to focus the program's goals on high-risk youth, thus merging the two important causes. Notwithstanding the newly released White House statement that Mrs. Reagan would enter the Naval Hospital in Bethesda that evening in preparation for a biopsy on her left breast, she remained focused on her agenda and friendly with the crowd. Maintaining her commitment to Foster Grandparents, in spite of the frightening personal challenges that lay ahead, earned her the respect of many that day. "What she did here today is a model for adults to live by and children to learn from," praised Dennis Harrington, the principal of Maplewood.

The first lady interacts with a classroom of program participants at Maplewood Elementary School.

OPPOSITE: Wool suit, with cashmere sweater gathered at the shoulder and leather belt, designed by Oscar de la Renta.

**OUTREACH TO CHILDREN**  Through her commitment to Foster Grandparents, Nancy Reagan spent many hours in hospitals and clinics and, by extension, visiting ailing children across the nation. Every Christmas she delivered toys to the Children's Hospital in Washington. She traveled to St. Ann's Infant Home in Maryland and to Columbia Presbyterian Medical Center in New York City. In 1983 her concern for young people brought her to another country, South Korea, and to two small children in particular, Ahn Ji Sook and Lee Kil Woo. Just seven and four years old, respectively, both children suffered from holes in the lower chambers of their hearts. In November of that year, President and Mrs. Reagan traveled to South Korea and brought the children back to the United States for open-heart surgery. A month later, as they were on the mend, the first lady paid them a visit at St. Francis Hospital in Roslyn, New York. "They look wonderful," she proclaimed. "This is Thanksgiving and Christmas all wrapped into one." "I love you," the seven year old said with a hug. And she gave Mrs. Reagan a Christmas card in which she had written, "Thank you for all you have done to save my life."

LEFT: Wool plaid suit, designed by Yves Saint Laurent.

RIGHT: On March 18, 1981, Mrs. Reagan supports the Foster Grandparents program at St. Ann's Infant Home in Hyattsville, Maryland.

TOP: In October 1982, Mrs. Reagan
hosts a special luncheon on the
White House South Lawn and
Frank Sinatra performs his single
"To Love a Child."

BOTTOM: Mrs. Reagan plays with
Lee Kil Woo and Ahn Ji Sook
in Korea, before bringing them to
America for open-heart surgery.

# LEADING THE "JUST SAY NO" CAMPAIGN

*Drugs take away the dream from every child's heart*
*and replace it with a nightmare, and it's time we in America*
*stand up and replace those dreams.*

— NANCY REAGAN

Nancy Reagan has shown that the president is not the only one who can use that "bully pulpit" for the good of America.

While she was involved in the anti-drug cause before reaching the White House, by 1982, the first lady had embraced the campaign with energy and evident feeling. A name for her cause was chosen after she met with schoolchildren in Oakland. "A little girl raised her hand," she remembered, "and said, 'Mrs. Reagan, what do you do if somebody offers you drugs?' And I said, 'well, you just say no.' And there it was born. I think people thought we had an advertising agency over who dreamed that up—not true."

By 1988 more than 12,000 "Just Say No" clubs had been formed across the country and around the world. As the captain in her crusade for a drug-free America, she inspired millions to stand up and join her. The results were encouraging: cocaine use by high-school seniors dropped by one-third, from 6.2 percent in 1986 to 4.3 percent in 1987, the lowest level in a decade. More than 10 percent of the members of the class of 1978 said they used marijuana daily, but by 1987 the figure was only about 3 percent among high-school seniors.

The crusade made serious demands on her time: 110 appearances and fourteen anti-drug speeches in 1984 alone. "The kids relate to me and I to them," she

On March 22, 1982, Mrs. Reagan organizes the first White House
conference of first ladies from around the world to discuss drug abuse and families.
OPPOSITE: The first lady hosts a White House reception for the presentation
of *Newsweek* magazine's special edition on the drug crisis on January 21, 1987.

said. Her intense effort to fight school-age drug and alcohol abuse took her to sixty-five cities in thirty-three states and nine foreign countries. To create greater awareness of the crisis, the first lady played herself on an episode of the situation comedy "Diff'rent Strokes," was cohost of "Good Morning America," narrated an anti-drug documentary for PBS, *The Chemical People*, and participated in thirty-eight special radio and TV tapings. She also invited the spouses of two dozen heads of state to a three-day anti-drug forum in Washington and Atlanta.

"Nancy has devoted herself in these last few years to the battle against drug abuse," her husband announced, "and I'm very proud of everything she's doing in this truly noble endeavor. And she's been promoting one method of fighting drug abuse that may have some application to the battle for tax reform. . . . And so, I hope you'll take this message to members of Congress concerning this tax proposal. Tell them when the special interests come around they should 'Just say no.'"

In 1986, when the president signed a proclamation creating the first official "Just Say No to Drugs Week," Nancy Reagan spoke from the heart when she said, "Someone asked me if I wanted to make a New Year's wish, and I said yes—and it was that I'd like to see every young person in the world join the 'Just Say No' to drugs club. Well, just the fact that Congress has proclaimed 'Just Say No Week' and in light of all the activities taking place, it seems that my wish is well on its way to coming true."

On May 13, 1987, Mrs. Reagan joins a televised "Just Say No" rally
with Soleil Moon Frye (a.k.a. Punky Brewster) at Universal City, California.

TOP: Children rally at the White House on May 22, 1986,
in a show of support for Mrs. Reagan's anti-drug campaign.
BOTTOM: Mrs. Reagan break-dances with youth at
Covenant House in New York City on June 18, 1985.

**NANCY REAGAN TENNIS TOURNAMENT** "Semi-lawless tennis" is what the press called it. And with Mr. T as the referee, that is not hard to envision. The first lady wore this linen Yves Saint Laurent ensemble to the second annual Nancy Reagan Drug Abuse Fund Tennis Tournament held on the White House courts. The Community Foundation of Greater Washington sponsored the fundraising event on May 24, 1986. With 250 spectators, and celebrities like Tom Selleck and Dorothy Hamill, the four-hour tournament was a rousing success. At the conclusion of the final match, Mrs. Reagan presented $100,000 to the "Just Say No" club and the Washington Fund for the Prevention of Substance Abuse. Later, in 1987, she recalled that when she began her anti-drug campaign five years earlier, "No one was enthusiastic about my getting involved in the drug problem. They thought it was too grim and depressing." Clearly, the first lady demonstrated that she could bring fun and uplifting rewards to those who would support a "grim and depressing" but very important cause.

Linen suit with scoop neck and matching belt, designed by Yves Saint Laurent.

OPPOSITE: The Reagans cross the White House tennis court to welcome guests to the 1986 Nancy Reagan Tennis Tournament.

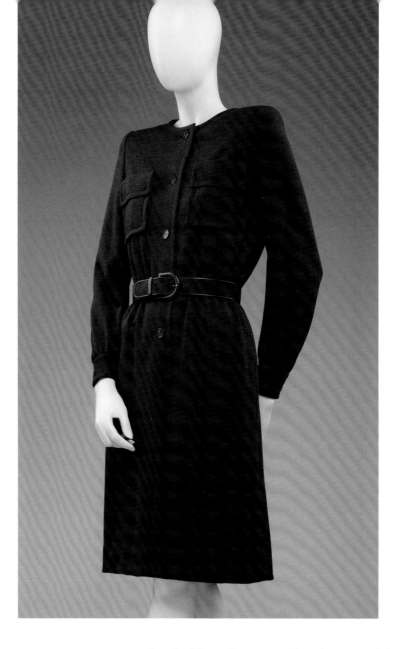

Knit jersey day dress with patch pockets, designed by Bill Blass.

OPPOSITE: With a little help from the NBA's Wayman Tisdale and Charles Barkley, Mrs. Reagan shoots two out of three at Market Square Arena in Indianapolis, Indiana.

**ATHLETES JUST SAY "NO"** Nancy Reagan was keenly aware of the influence athletes were having on young people and believed that if she could attain their public endorsement, she could reach more people with her anti-drug message. In 1988, she enlisted the support of four major sports leagues, beginning with the NBA. On February 4, she was the star of the half-time show, in this knit Bill Blass dress worn as a tunic with a slim-fitting leather skirt underneath, at the Indiana Pacers–Philadelphia 76ers game. It was "Just Say No" Night, and twenty-two teams in eleven cities were devoting their half-time shows to Nancy Reagan's anti-drug message. Wayman Tisdale of the Pacers and Charles Barkley of the 76ers hoisted Mrs. Reagan upward as she shot two out of three baskets for the cause. Then, it was the NHL's turn. Twenty-one teams championed the "Just Say No" Foundation in a weeklong tribute. In Landover, Maryland, taking cues from the Philadelphia Flyers and the Washington Capitals, she made two out of three goals. By October, the NFL and Major League Baseball got on board with the program.

Taking her anti-drug message to the big leagues, Mrs. Reagan tosses the first pitch at Dodgers Stadium for the 1988 World Series, in which the A's played the Dodgers, in Los Angeles, California.

OPPOSITE: Taking pointers from the National Hockey League at the Capital Centre near Washington, D.C., Mrs. Reagan scores two out of three for "Just Say No" on March 25, 1988.

*As first lady, you will be the object of attention no matter what you do.*
*So I decided I might as well focus the attention on something that*
*really mattered, on something that had interested me for a long time.*

— NANCY REAGAN

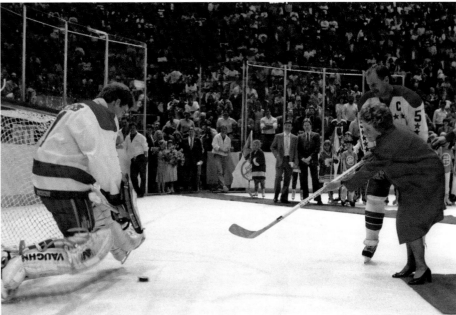

*The first time I received a letter saying that I had saved a person's life, I wept. I never dreamed I had the ability to do that— to influence people who were unknown to me.*

— NANCY REAGAN, 1988

**INTERNATIONAL DRUG-ABUSE EFFORTS**   On October 20, 1988, with her husband by her side, Mrs. Reagan wore this Adolfo suit when she graciously accepted the recognition given her by Kiwanis International, Covenant House, Boy Scouts of America, the NBA, the NHL, and twenty-five other groups for drawing international attention to the drug problem among our youth. Special guests included Frank Gifford, as master of ceremonies, and Bob Hope. Also participating was Robin Page, whose poignant letter describing her difficult life as a teenage addict had deeply affected the wives of world leaders attending the 1985 White House Conference. In a tearful moment of gratitude, Ms. Page said, "I owe my life to a lot of people, and very much to you for making such a big impression." Pope John Paul II also extended his "sincere appreciation." In a letter sent on his behalf from the Apostolic Pro-Nuncio, he wrote of Nancy Reagan, "[Y]our endeavors in this critical area are most effective and enlightened," and "your luminous example has encouraged countless others." With spotlights around the world now focused on "Just Say No," her example was luminous indeed.

Mrs. Reagan thanks Bob Hope while Frank Gifford presides over the Kiwanis International Dinner at the Shoreham Hotel.

OPPOSITE: Brocade evening suit with peplum detail, designed by Adolfo.

*It became a rallying point. You saw it on milk cartons
and billboards, and you still hear it used today. I've always been
proud of that, and of the work we did.*

— NANCY REAGAN

Wool suit with contrasting ribbed satin Peter Pan collar and belt.

RIGHT: President and Mrs. Reagan receive the White House Drug Study Report from Secretary Otis Bowen on January 14, 1988, in the West Sitting Hall of the White House.

OPPOSITE: Mrs. Reagan sits with the press: (clockwise from top right) Diane Sawyer in the Map Room of the White House on October 26, 1982; Mike Wallace in the Center Sitting Hall of the White House on January 6, 1989; Merv Griffin on the set of his show in Los Angeles on October 6, 1982; Ted Koppel in the Red Room of the White House on February 29, 1988; and Barbara Walters in the Yellow Oval Room of the White House Residence on May 18, 1981.

**HIGH-SCHOOL DRUG-ABUSE STUDY**  In a radio address to the nation given on January 16, 1988, President Reagan announced, "My fellow Americans: This week something happened here in Washington that makes me proud, and I expect you'll feel the same way." He was referring to the results of the annual report that measured high school seniors' attitudes about drug use, which Dr. Otis Bowen, the Secretary of Health and Human Services, had presented to President and Mrs. Reagan two days earlier at the White House. Mrs. Reagan wore this attractive black and red Valentino dress to the presentation of the study. For the first time in thirteen years—when the survey began—the results showed a substantial change in teens' attitudes. Significantly fewer high-school seniors than ever before reported using cocaine or marijuana, and many more students than ever acknowledged that drug use was dangerous. "Students are no longer buying the old line that experimenting with cocaine and other illegal drugs is safe," the president continued. "Just Say No" was clearly making an impact.

# PRIVATE MOMENTS
# IN A PUBLIC OFFICE

*My darling, here it is, our day. If we were home,*
*we would have a fire and funnies. And we would hate*
*anybody who called or dropped in.*

— RONALD REAGAN

The Reagans dine on television trays in the
president's study at the White House on November 6, 1981.
OPPOSITE: President and Mrs. Reagan take their
new anniversary toy for a spin at Rancho del Cielo.
PAGE 208: The president and first lady embrace at
Rancho del Cielo in Santa Barbara, California.

A good friend of Ronald and Nancy Reagan's observed that he was always glad to come home. "He knew Nancy would be there, waiting for him with open arms. To be treasured like that is a wonderful, wonderful thing."

A loyal advisor to the Reagans for many years, Nancy Reynolds expressed her immense respect for Nancy Reagan's ability to create a loving home: "They really wanted to be private people. They loved being alone. . . . When he came in that door after a terrible day with the legislature, there were always flowers and a wonderful, quiet meal, with no telephone going off. I think he was enormously grateful to Nancy for creating this wonderful sanctuary."

Even at the White House, the two busiest people in America were determined to carve out private time, and Mrs. Reagan tastefully converted their formal surroundings into a home. Although a bit shabby and tired when they arrived, the White House was transformed by the new first lady into pristine condition.

"I'll never forget how, right after the renovations were done, one of the butlers who had been there a long, long time looked down the hall and said, 'This is how the White House should look.' That was one of my proudest moments as first lady. It was my Oscar."

She warmed up their bedroom with wallpaper in an eighteenth-century print and salmon-colored carpeting. The President's Bedroom, or "study," as her husband called it, was brightened with rich red carpeting, upholstery, and drapes. Photographs filled the room. It was their favorite hideaway for sharing the news of the day while watching the sunset over the Potomac. And, of course, always present were simple, elegant flower arrangements with lots of white or fragrant flowers like lilies of the valley, roses, lilacs, tuberoses, peonies, and sweet peas.

Ronald Reagan described his bride well when he wrote, "There is a gal I love who is a nest builder. If she were stuck three days in a hotel room, she'd manage to make it home sweet home."

But as much as Ronald and Nancy Reagan loved the White House, they "felt like a bird in a gilded cage, and they don't open the door very often to let the bird out. . . . Thank God for Camp David!" Nancy Reagan exclaimed. "I never expected that we would use it practically every weekend, but it became a regular and wel-

come part of our routine." Its secluded setting and rustic charm also ensured that any changes she made to the decor were not on the White House press corps radar screen. The Reagans converted the paved roads, originally installed for Richard Nixon's golf cart, to trails suitable for horseback riding.

Sometimes they would travel to Camp David via helicopter and sometimes they would just "drive off—almost like ordinary people." But no matter what, "When you're president, there's no such thing as a vacation," Nancy said. "No matter where you go, there are always briefing books to study, papers to read, intelligence reports to review, speeches to work on, decisions to be made. You might be in the mountains but you're still president and the world doesn't stop turning."

Bathed in sunlight while fog hugged the shoreline below, Rancho del Cielo, or "Ranch in the Sky," in Santa Barbara was their cherished hideaway. "Ronnie is so happy there! He loves to be outside, building fences, cutting down trees and brush. . . . When you get up there, the rest of the world disappears." He threw himself into remodeling the old one-story adobe house to make it comfortable for Nancy, who pitched in with all the chores. "I'm crazy about the girl who goes to the ranch with me," wrote Ronald Reagan. "If we're tidying up the woods she's a pee-wee power house at pushing over dead trees. She's a wonderful person to sit by the fire with."

Mrs. Reagan shares a quiet moment with the president
in the Oval Office on her birthday, July 6, 1986.

Whether in Ronnie's study in the White House, in their private rooms aboard Air Force One, or by the fireplace at Rancho del Cielo, the Reagans love was here to stay. "It was the real deal," said White House photographer Pete Souza.

There were beautiful love letters, some composed by the president and some from his "roommate." As their good friend Merv Griffin said, "It's the private part of their life that really none of us, even the friends, knew, except they were in love. But we had no idea there existed these letters."

Such expressions of love extended to their delight in celebrating each other's birthdays. Ronald Reagan even sent flowers to his mother-in-law, Edith Davis, on Nancy's birthday to thank her for giving birth to his beloved wife, the woman who, in his words, "made his life complete." In 1983, Nancy really caught her "roommate" by surprise as she rolled out a birthday cake right in the middle of a press conference on domestic and foreign policy issues. The entire press corps, led by Mrs. Reagan, sang "Happy Birthday," and when he blew out the candles, they asked him, "Did you wish for a balanced budget, Mr. President?" to which he replied, "You can't tell what you wished or it won't come true." The Reagans escaped to Camp David for a party with friends, beautifully orchestrated by the "First Mommie" for the "First Poppa."

Mrs. Reagan always said, "If Ronnie and I hadn't been so close, I don't know how we would have weathered the many . . . experiences we had during the White House years. They run through my mind now—the shooting, the deaths of my father and mother, my breast cancer, Ronnie's colon and prostate cancer." Life was not always easy at 1600 Pennsylvania Avenue. But, Nancy said, "Through it all, the journey has truly been grand—for I have had the joy of traveling with my beloved companion, Ronald Reagan."

Mrs. Reagan takes the president home to recuperate from the attempt on his life when he is released from the George Washington University Hospital on April 11, 1981.

**BIRTHDAYS** "I.T.W.W.W." was how Ronald Reagan signed his wife's birthday cards. It stood for "In the Whole Wide World," as in, "I love you more than anything in the whole wide world." And often he gave her more than one card at a time. The Reagans always gave thoughtful attention to each other's birthdays, no matter what else was going on in their busy lives. In the 1960s, it became a tradition for Mrs. Reagan to share her birthday with family and old friends in an annual barbecue bash, and this continued during her husband's presidency. And, of course, there were celebrations with White House friends too. Mrs. Reagan wore this linen Valentino blouse and skirt to her birthday party with White House staff in 1986. With the president's birthday falling on February 6, his parties were usually in the White House. Nancy Reagan always found special ways of celebrating, publicly and privately, whether by turning a press briefing into a surprise birthday party or by joining with friends to throw a private celebration in the White House.

Linen blouse and matching skirt, designed by Valentino.

Mrs. Reagan spends a belated birthday celebration with her staff at Clyde's Restaurant on July 7, 1986.

LEFT: On February 7, 1986, the Reagans' longtime friends held a private dinner in the White House to celebrate the president's seventy-fifth birthday. President Reagan poses with his wife and "Kitchen Cabinet" friends Betty and William Wilson, Earle Jorgensen, Armand and Harriet Deutsch, Marion Jorgensen, and Leonore Annenberg.

FOLLOWING PAGES: On February 4, 1983, Mrs. Reagan surprises the president—and the press corps—with a cake during a White House briefing two days before his seventy-second birthday.

TOP: The first lady receives a warm welcome home to the White House after her radical mastectomy in 1987.

BOTTOM: In July 1985, the president waves to supporters upon his return to the White House after his cancer surgery.

RIGHT: Wool knit jersey day dress with suede belt, designed by Oscar de la Renta.

Mrs. Reagan poses with representatives of the American Cancer Society after a special taping on February 19, 1988, four months after undergoing breast cancer surgery.

**THE AMERICAN CANCER SOCIETY**   Nancy Reagan wore this Oscar de la Renta day dress to a taping for the American Cancer Society on February 19, 1988. She had been a longtime supporter of the organization, having served previously as its honorary chair and presenter of the Courage Award. Then, in 1988, she was honored with the Courage Award, along with sixty other recipients, after her own bout with cancer. President Reagan presided over the ceremony. In gratitude, Mrs. Reagan poignantly remarked, "I can't say that it's an award that I dreamed of getting when I was growing up, but that's what happens sometimes in life," and she expressed her hope that sharing her experience publicly had helped others. The Reagans faced many personal challenges while in the White House. Among them was Nancy Reagan's modified radical mastectomy on October 17, 1987. She had barely recuperated when, just nine days later, her beloved mother, Edie Davis, died. Such personal challenges are difficult for anyone, and yet, with stoicism and grace, Mrs. Reagan triumphed over these hardships in front of a nation of onlookers.

*It was impressed upon us from the beginning that Camp David was the president's most private retreat, and that every other president has gone to great lengths to keep it that way. So did we.*

— NANCY REAGAN

Fur-lined canvas coat.

OPPOSITE: President and Mrs. Reagan depart the South Lawn for relaxation at Camp David on January 22, 1982.

**CAMP DAVID** This warm trench coat was a staple for those wintry days heading to Camp David. Nancy Reagan was frequently photographed in it, as she and her husband boarded the Marine One helicopter for their ride to the presidential retreat. Shangri-la, as President Roosevelt had called it, was a secluded sanctuary for the Reagans where they could safely enjoy the outdoors and restful activities without an entourage. As Nancy Reagan described it, "What we really enjoyed doing there was relaxing, wearing blue jeans, reading, riding horses, watching movies—just generally doing the kinds of things that we'd always done on the ranch back home." The only thing it seemed to lack was a chapel. If President and Mrs. Reagan wanted to attend services they would have to take the whole Secret Service entourage with them, which they felt "didn't seem right." So, before departing the White House, the Reagans put in motion plans for construction of a chapel, which was completed while George H. W. Bush was president.

*I love the whole gang of you—Mommie, first lady, the sentimental you, the fun you and the peewee power house you . . . Merry Christmas you all.*

Mrs. Reagan wraps Christmas gifts in the Private Residence of the White House in 1981.

RIGHT: Silk blouse with front knife pleats and matching wide-leg pleated pants, embellished with velvet and faux jewels at the collar, cuffs, and hip, designed by Adolfo.

On Christmas Eve, 1987, Mrs. Reagan takes her brother's family on a tour of the White House Christmas decorations.

**CHRISTMAS WITH FAMILY AND FRIENDS**   "In some ways our Christmas at the White House is not all that different from our California Christmas. It just seems to come naturally to me to make it the way it always has been," Nancy Reagan explained. That meant not only adorning the White House in old-fashioned decorations but also maintaining the celebratory traditions that she and her husband had been enjoying for years. On December 24, 1987, Mrs. Reagan wore this silk ensemble to the home of the Reagans' good friends Charles and Mary Jane Wick, after guiding her brother's family on a tour of the White House Christmas decorations. Traditionally, Christmas Eve was spent at the Wicks' home, often with both families' children and grandchildren. The Wicks would always pick someone to play Santa Claus, and the selection would remain a secret until it was time to pull on the red suit and pillows. Even the first lady had her turn. Mrs. Reagan would then host the group at the White House on Christmas Day, serving turkey, dressing, potatoes, and, of course, her family's traditional monkey bread. But one of Nancy Reagan's most cherished holiday traditions was the sentimental Christmas letter she would receive from her "roommate."

224

*Nancy Reagan has a sense of style like no other. Very few first ladies represented American fashion in the manner that she did. . . . I was very proud to dress her.*

— OSCAR DE LA RENTA, 2007

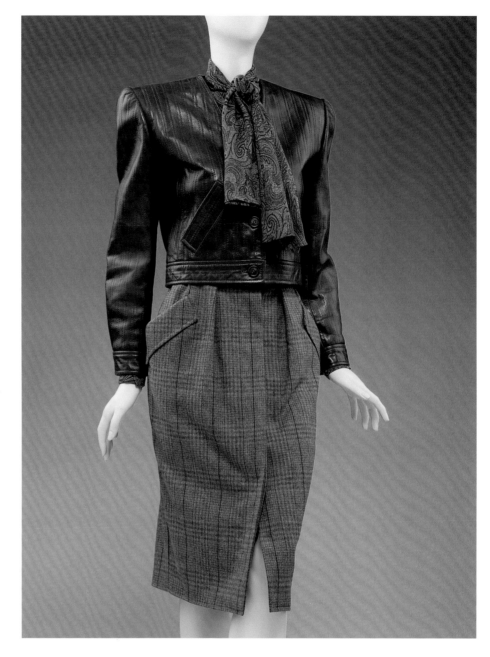

Leather jacket with coordinating silk paisley blouse and plaid wool skirt, designed by Oscar de la Renta.

OPPOSITE: The president and first lady break ground on a hilltop in Simi Valley, California, for construction of the Ronald Reagan Presidential Library and Museum.

**THE RONALD REAGAN PRESIDENTIAL LIBRARY**   On a majestic peak in Simi Valley, California, with resplendent views of the valleys below, President and Mrs. Reagan dug into the earth with their shiny silver shovels. The date was November 21, 1988, and the site was to become the home of the Ronald Reagan Presidential Library and Museum. The first lady was fashionably attired in this leather jacket with a plaid skirt and coordinating paisley blouse, all designed by Oscar de la Renta. In his dedication remarks, the president noted, "This is a most humbling moment for me. This Library will allow scholars of the future to cast their own judgment on these years, and I would not presume to predict the result of their research." It was Thanksgiving weekend, and after the ceremony the president and first lady continued on to their ranch to celebrate the holiday with friends and family. The Library opened to much fanfare three years later, on November 4, 1991.

**RANCHO DEL CIELO, SANTA BARBARA**    The Reagans purchased their
688-acre ranch with a small adobe home while Ronald Reagan was still governor
of California. With the help of friends, the couple immediately "knocked out walls,
laid new tile floors, painted the house," and generally made it livable. While he
painted fences and chopped wood, she decorated with Mexican rugs and wicker
chairs, turning the interiors of a "tiny two-bedroom house" into a cozy haven.
Nearby Lake Lucky was home to their canoe, called TruLuv, which Ronald Reagan
had given to his wife on their silver anniversary.

President and Mrs. Reagan go
horseback riding at Rancho del
Cielo on August 15, 1983.

*From the first day we saw it,*
*Rancho del Cielo cast a spell over us.*

— RONALD REAGAN

Mrs. Reagan cuddles with one of
the ranch's dogs.

TOP: Mrs. Reagan cools off at the
ranch with an ice cream cone.

BOTTOM: The Reagans enjoy a
relaxing lunch at the ranch on
April 8, 1985.

# DEPARTURES

# LEAVING WASHINGTON

*May only good and wise men inhabit this house.*

— JOHN ADAMS

They were familiar with every room and hallway. They had the warmest memories of their life in that historic mansion, yet now it was time to depart. While Ronald Reagan was giving speeches recounting his triumphs, his "roommate" was wrestling with an exit strategy: where to live and how to get there. Just try to bring the president of the United States with you while house hunting in nosy Southern California. Nancy Reagan managed to pull this off by smuggling her husband out of a hotel and into a nearby vehicle, then asking him to hide on the floor of the car. They cruised up to the house, he popped up for a quick look, signaled his approval, then went back undercover. "I had to find a way for him to see it without the press catching on," she said. "I didn't think that was the best way to make friends with the neighbors, either."

Back in Washington, she made arrangements for the move and stood by her husband's side through all the goodbyes. "Nothing can prepare you for living in the White House—and nothing can prepare you for leaving it," she said. "Our final two months were emotionally and physically draining." There were honors levied by the Senate, by Walter Cronkite at the Kennedy Center, by the White House press corps. The Children's Hospital named a room for Nancy because of all her visits there. For their last Christmas weekend at Camp David, their cabin had been decorated more beautifully than ever, and at dinner they were serenaded by Christmas carols.

For the first lady, leaving the "house" where she had made so many changes was not easy, either. "I put a lot into that house, and I was leaving a lot of me there." Nancy Reagan would also miss the magnolia trees she planted. "My heart ached as I looked at those beautiful grounds that I was unlikely to see again."

The final day was dismal, emotionally and symbolically, with gray, cold skies hovering over the ceremonies. The excitement of inauguration day swirled about them. Following the inauguration, "The Bushes and Quayles walked down the steps to see us off in the helicopter. . . . When we took off, the pilots circled the White House so we could see it once more, and Ronnie leaned over to me and said, 'Look, dear, there's our bungalow.' This was really goodbye to Washington and eight, wonderful, exciting, frustrating, and sometimes frightening years."

America's thirty-seventh first lady said she learned how to serve and how "to go on being myself . . . for this and for so many other things, I'll always be grateful."

OPPOSITE: Boarding Marine One as private citizens on January 20, 1989, the
Reagans depart the U.S. Capitol after the presidential inauguration of George H. W. Bush.
PAGE 230: The president and first lady stand in the Entrance Hall
of the White House on the president's last day in office, January 20, 1989.

*Over the past eight years in the White House, I have found how to serve. And for that I will be forever grateful to the American people.*

— NANCY REAGAN, 1988

Titled a "hero" by the president in his last State of the Union Address, Mrs. Reagan accepts the applause graciously.

OPPOSITE: Double-breasted wool crepe suit with satin trim, by Chanel.

**SALUTING THE HERO**   Nancy Reagan wore this Chanel suit to President Reagan's last State of the Union address on January 25, 1988. At almost every State of the Union address he gave, the president had recognized an ordinary person who had achieved a great act—"heroes" he called them. The person he honored in his final address had, by many accounts, achieved a great deal. "The war against drugs is a war of individual battles, a crusade with so many heroes—including America's young people," he said, "and also someone very special to me. She has helped many of our young people to say 'no' to drugs. Nancy, much credit belongs to you, and I want to express to you your husband's pride and your country's thanks." And with humble surprise, Nancy Reagan graciously accepted the president's recognition. "Surprised you, didn't I?" he concluded as he blew her a kiss.

**THE PRESIDENT'S DINNER**   On May 11, 1988, wearing this lace Oscar de la
Renta gown, the first lady attended the President's Dinner, an annual Republican
congressional fundraising event, at which President Reagan announced his formal
support of George H. W. Bush for president. It was one of the first major public
appearances Mrs. Reagan made after her breast cancer surgery. When, in a sponta-
neous show of solidarity, the Reagans and Bushes joined hands high above their
heads, the president had forgotten the need to be a little more delicate with his
wife's tender arm. She was stoic initially, but, as the enthusiasm continued, she
finally whispered to him, "You're hurting me," prompting the president's loving
apology: a kiss on her forehead.

The president apologizes
with a kiss.

Satin evening gown with sweetheart
neck and embroidered lace overlay,
designed by Oscar de la Renta.

ABOVE: Detail of the embroidered
sleeve.

**1988 REPUBLICAN CONVENTION**   This silk Adolfo dress was lucky for Nancy Reagan. She wore it to both the 1980 and 1988 Republican conventions. Of course, the main purpose of the 1988 convention in New Orleans was to nominate a new presidential candidate. However, it was also a time for the president and first lady to bid farewell. Wearing this soft pink dress to the Superdome on August 15, 1988, the first lady stood before a sea of delegates and extended her heartfelt gratitude: "I want to thank you for all the years you've worked on our behalf. I'll miss you. I'll never forget you. Thank you for all you have done for me." Earlier that day, at the New Orleans Convention Center, the delegates hosted a special "thank you" of their own. To her surprise, President Reagan appeared, and brought tears to her eyes with his touching remarks: "Nancy, in front of all your friends here today, let me say, thank you for all you do, thank you for your love, and thank you for just being you."

The president and first lady wave to delegates at the New Orleans convention.

OPPOSITE LEFT: Pleated silk day dress with necktie and slender sash, designed by Adolfo.

OPPOSITE RIGHT: Mrs. Reagan waves good-bye.

*Our time at center stage is over.*

— NANCY REAGAN, 1988

**THE LIFETIME ACHIEVEMENT AWARD**    At its first-ever awards dinner, held in 1984, the Council of Fashion Designers of America (CFDA) invited Nancy Reagan to serve as its honorary chair as they honored James Galanos. The council invited her back as its honorary chair for the following three dinners as well. Then in 1988, the CFDA paid tribute to Mrs. Reagan with a Lifetime Achievement Award. In her touching presentation of the award, Barbara Walters declared not only that Mrs. Reagan's support of American designers "stimulates the fashion industry, it hurts no one, and it adds to our pride in American clothes," but also that, given their position, first ladies ought to encourage fashionable dress.

Oscar de la Renta and Barbara Walters pose with the honoree.

OPPOSITE: Congratulations are bestowed from designers Carolina Herrera, Bill Blass, and Oscar de la Renta.

*She has a marvelous awareness of what is appropriate for her as
first lady. . . . I think one of the things that Nancy Reagan has tried
to emphasize . . . is that the role of first lady does demand
a certain dignity and a certain style, not only in dressing but in
attitude. She's a master at that. She's, well, representing our
nation. And for that, I think, bravo for looking well.*

— BILL BLASS, 1984

# THE PRESIDENT'S FUNERAL

*Living without Ronnie is unthinkable.*

— NANCY REAGAN

When the Ronald Reagan Presidential Library was dedicated in 1991, the former president and his first lady chose it as their final resting place, inspired by its quiet dignity and beautiful vistas.

Nancy Reagan never wanted to be anyplace except by her husband's side. The woman who stood with him through his rise and tended to him during his decline faced a week of difficult ceremonies as she prepared to say goodbye to her husband, who passed away on June 5, 2004. Unquestionably, her last commitment was to lay him to rest and to allow the public to have a chance to pay their respects.

At the final moment, when his breathing was labored, he opened his eyes and gazed straight at his loving wife. His eyes were clear and blue and full of love. It was "the greatest gift" he could have given her.

A dear family friend expressed the concern of millions of Americans. "I don't know how she did it. I just—we all prayed for her. We all thought about her." The ceremonies began as Nancy Reagan, slow in step, shepherded the casket with quiet intensity, turning the most public of events into a series of private moments.

First, her husband lay in repose at the Ronald Reagan Presidential Library, where more than 100,000 mourners paid their respects in a thirty-four-hour vigil. Handling everything with selfless grace and dignity, Mrs. Reagan then accompanied the casket aboard the current Air Force One aircraft, traveling to Washington where the rotunda of the Capitol would provide another opportunity for Americans to say farewell to the fortieth president.

The procession from Andrews Air Force Base to the Capitol stunned Mrs. Reagan. While she privately grieved for her husband's loss, the public outpouring along the fourteen-mile route overwhelmed her. Boy Scouts in khaki shorts waving flags and saluting, office workers with ID tags around their necks in tears, tourists holding signs "You'll Always Be Our First Lady," and "We Love You, Nancy"—it was a visual spectacle embracing her husband and the woman who loved him. And they did not even know him. "I think they broke the mold when they made Ronnie," she said.

In the Capitol rotunda ceremony, Mrs. Reagan caressed the flag-covered coffin and rested her head against it lovingly, opening the way for dignitaries who arrived from around the world.

The president and first lady share a bench on the South Lawn in October 1988.

While Americans paid their respects at the Capitol, Mrs. Reagan accepted visitors at Blair House. Even Mikhail Gorbachev came. "He's been so sweet to me. . . . He stood there at the door and I looked up and there he was with his arms outstretched. And I went over to him and he hugged me. And we just stood there. It was so sweet." The first to see Mrs. Reagan, Margaret Thatcher, wrote in the condolence book, "To Ronnie: Well done, thou good and faithful servant."

Services at the National Cathedral saluted not only the president but also his wife. "We seek to comfort you," President Bush explained, "to tell you of our admiration for your courage and your selfless caring." Former Canadian Prime Minister Brian Mulroney recalled when Nancy and his wife, Mila, stepped out of a car looking "like a million bucks. . . . President Reagan beamed, threw his arm around my shoulder and said with a grin, 'You know, Brian, for two Irishmen, we sure married up!'"

*Ronald Reagan's life was rich not only in public achievement,*
*but also in private happiness. Indeed, his public achievements were*
*rooted in his private happiness. The great turning point of his*
*life was his meeting and marriage with Nancy.*

— LADY MARGARET THATCHER, JUNE 2004

Lady Margaret Thatcher comforts Mrs. Reagan at Blair House.

Bells at churches around the nation rang forty times in honor of the nation's fortieth president, and for three minutes Las Vegas lost its glimmer as casino lights dimmed.

The long, final trip to California ended with a memorable sunset burial service at the Reagan Library. Mrs. Reagan embraced the mahogany casket one more time, pressing her cheek against its cool surface, and whispered a final word. For the first time during a week of mourning, she seemed on the verge of losing her composure, tears welling in her eyes.

Her husband was buried beneath a presidential memorial at the Library. A curved granite wall frames the memorial and is inscribed with Ronald Reagan's words:

*I know in my heart that man is good.*
*That what is right will always eventually triumph.*
*And there is purpose and worth to each and every life.*

LEFT: Wool suit with satin trim and a pair of brooches, designed by James Galanos.
RIGHT: Mrs. Reagan receives a hug from Mikhail Gorbachev at Blair House.

Mrs. Reagan awaits the president's draped casket on the U.S. Capitol steps.

*I try to remember Ronnie telling me so many times that God
has a plan for us which we don't understand now but one day will,
or my mother saying that you play the hand that's dealt you. It's
hard but even now there are moments that Ronnie has given me that
I wouldn't trade for anything. Alzheimer's is a truly long, long
goodbye. But it's the living out of love.*

— NANCY REAGAN

In the rotunda of the U.S. Capitol, the first lady kisses her husband's casket.

# CONCLUSION

## A LEGACY OF LOVE AND DEDICATION

### BOB COLACELLO

About halfway into President Reagan's first term, one of Mrs. Reagan's aides asked her if she ever thought of her place in history. "Oh, no," the first lady responded without a moment's hesitation. "It's Ronnie's place in history I think about." Eighteen years have passed since Ronald and Nancy Reagan left the White House and retired to their new house on a hill overlooking Los Angeles. Thirteen years have passed since the former president told the American people—in perhaps the most eloquent letter ever written by a public figure about a private matter—that he had been diagnosed with Alzheimer's. It has been three years since he succumbed to that cruel disease. Through everything, Nancy Reagan has never stopped serving him—and the nation—with the same elegance, strength, and dignity that she brought to her eight years as first lady. In doing so, she has not only assured his place in history, but her own.

As her husband's illness took hold, she stayed by his side, supervising his care, guarding his privacy, comforting him as best she could. Defying the expectations of those critics who had always miscast her as a brittle socialite mainly interested in shopping and parties, she turned down invitations to large public affairs and relied on the suits and dresses in her closet to see her through the few social obligations she continued to fulfill. When she ventured out to lunch with a pal or two it was almost always at the Hotel Bel Air, five minutes from home. At small dinners at the homes of close friends, she was always the first to leave, anxious to get back to her Ronnie. Wherever she went, people approached her, to thank her for taking such good care of the president or to tell her they, too, had a family member suffering from Alzheimer's and knew how heartbreaking it was to watch a loved one fade away.

On the extremely rare occasion that she put on an evening gown—or traveled out of town—it was to represent her ailing husband or honor his legacy. In 1996, at the Republican National Convention in San Diego, she gave her first speech on his behalf; four years later, she spoke at the party's convention in Philadelphia. In 1998, she flew to Washington for the official dedication of the Ronald Reagan Building and International Trade Center and a fundraiser for the Ronald Reagan Institute of Emergency Medicine at George Washington University, held in the Reagan Building's soaring atrium. She wore a red Bill Blass suit for the afternoon

Nancy Reagan in the Rose Garden of the White House.

ceremony and a white-sequined Galanos sheath for the evening gala, and she looked so perfect in both that few would have guessed these outfits were from the 1980s. In 2001, on a wet March day in Newport News, Virginia, she christened the aircraft carrier USS *Ronald Reagan–CVN–76*, splashing champagne on her black raincoat—and President George W. Bush's gray suit. Two years later, she returned to Virginia on a sunny July day for the ship's commissioning at the Norfolk Naval Base and, wearing a crisp, white-cotton pantsuit, delivered those magical words, "Man the ship and bring her alive!" setting off an explosion of applause from the more than 20,000 onlookers. On each of these occasions, she ended her speech with the same poignant words: "I wish Ronnie could be here today. Somehow, I feel he is."

Mrs. Reagan's dedication to her husband's legacy is nowhere more evident than at the Ronald Reagan Presidential Library and Foundation. She has not only raised millions of dollars toward its endowment but also helped make it into a national forum for political discourse by personally inviting high-ranking public officials and distinguished intellectuals—former prime ministers Margaret Thatcher and Brian Mulroney, Chief Justice John Roberts, writer Walter Isaacson, and Secretary of State Condoleezza Rice, among many others—to speak on both her husband's presidency and current world affairs. She may be most proud of the Air Force One Pavilion, which houses the Boeing 707 that was used by President Reagan and six other presidents from 1972 to 2001, and which has attracted hundreds of thousands of new visitors to the museum since its installation in 2005. She must also be given credit for overseeing the publication of Ronald Reagan's writings, love letters, and personal diaries, all with the intent of illustrating his intelligence, sensitivity, and wisdom (while at the same time providing the Library with additional sources of revenue).

For many, Nancy Reagan's greatest gift to her husband was his funeral, a procession of moving ceremonies and services in Washington and California that in its simple grandeur allowed the nation to mourn a beloved leader with grace and style. Protocol dictated that all presidents begin planning for this final event even while still in office, and Nancy Reagan carried herself through it with a touching dignity, a widow in black who was having a hard time letting go of her loved one's casket. All the elements of Nancy Reagan's personal style—her code of conduct really—came together during those days: her respect for tradition, her understanding of symbolism, her attention to detail, her appreciation of beauty, her commitment to love.

In recent years, Nancy Reagan has taken up the controversial cause of embryonic stem-cell research, in the belief that it could lead to cures for Alzheimer's, Parkinson's, and other fatal diseases. She went public with her support at a 2004

Juvenile Diabetes Research Foundation dinner in Los Angeles, at which she accepted the organization's Caregiver Award. "Science has presented us with a hope called stem-cell research, which may provide our scientists with many answers that for so long have been beyond our grasp," she said. "I just don't see how we can turn our backs on this. We have lost so much time already. I really can't bear to lose anymore." Since then, she has worked with leading Republicans and Democrats in Congress, including Senators Orrin Hatch and Ted Kennedy, personally calling scores of senators and representatives and urging them to vote for a bill expanding federal financing of embryonic stem-cell research. Partly due to her efforts, Congress has passed this bill twice but fell short both times of the two-thirds majority needed to override President Bush's vetoes. One doubts that Mrs. Reagan will give up.

As Ronald Reagan's ranking among American presidents continues to rise in the estimation of a wide range of historians as well as the general public, so does Nancy Reagan's reputation as one of the nation's most gracious, hard-working, and effective first ladies. If his legacy can be painted in a few broad strokes of vibrant oils, hers might best be captured by a fine pencil drawing, perhaps dabbed with watercolors in sweet, pastel shades. He was the stubborn visionary who talked tough to the Soviets and won the Cold War, the forceful politician who slashed taxes and rejuvenated the economy, the charismatic leader who restored America's pride in itself and the world's faith in our good intentions.

Her achievements were subtler, harder to track because they were so intertwined with his, and therefore not so easily converted into simple pictures or phrases. She helped keep up the confidence and optimism on which his charisma was built; she created the atmosphere that eased his personal relationships with friends and foes alike, facilitating his diplomacy, furthering his political goals. She reached out socially to the Washington establishment of powerbrokers, pundits, and hostesses, helping them to see through the caricatures of her husband and to find the true value of the man. If it took people a little longer to realize her worth, she would live with that.

# AFTERWORD

As our first lady, Nancy Reagan always promoted American fashion. Whether wearing James Galanos, Oscar de la Renta, Bill Blass, Carolina Herrera, or her daily Adolfo suits, she put American fashion on an international level. Justifiably so, the CFDA gave her a Lifetime Achievement Award in 1988. Nancy Reagan will always be a symbol of American elegance and style and a significant contributor to American fashion.

DIANE VON FURSTENBERG
*President, Council of Fashion Designers of America*

Mrs. Reagan is given a Lifetime Achievement Award by the
Council of Fashion Designers of America for her support of American designers.

# ACKNOWLEDGMENTS

*Nancy Reagan—A First Lady's Style* would not have been possible without the collaboration and support of Mrs. Reagan and the Ronald Reagan Presidential Library Foundation. We are indebted to the chairman of the Foundation, Frederick J. Ryan, Jr., for his great assistance during the production of the catalogue and exhibition. We are particularly grateful to Duke Blackwood, Joanne Drake, Melissa Giller, and Wren Powell for their patience with our numerous requests, their extensive knowledge, and their professionalism, which made this experience a delight. Also, a very special acknowledgment goes to Kirby Hanson and Kate Holt, who contributed extensively to the research and writing of the catalogue. Their help has been immeasurable. This publication has also been greatly enhanced by the eloquent contribution of Bob Colacello. Special mention should be made of Diane von Furstenberg, president of the Council of Fashion Designers of America, whose afterword puts Mrs. Reagan's significance for American fashion design into perspective.

In addition, we would like to give a special thanks to the archival, curatorial, and Foundation staff for their invaluable assistance researching thousands of photographs and crucial information, especially Mike Duggan, Cate Sewell, Steve Branch, Ray Wilson, Shirley Short, Diane Barrie, Kelly Barton, Jenny Mandel, Lisa Jones, and Shelly Williams, who met every request for yet another image and historical research with patience and expediency. We greatly appreciate the tireless work of Thomas Thomas, Rob Zucca, Patti Marion, Carol Mann, Barbara Kurata, and Jennifer Torres, who meticulously cared for and archived Mrs. Reagan's dresses and helped on many levels with the execution of the catalogue and exhibition. We also thank Allison Borio, Jennifer Fornadley, Linda Hawa, Marguerite Jagard, and John Langellier, who displayed good humor and exceptional professionalism when presented with deadlines and last-minute requests.

We would also like to express our appreciation to James Galanos, who has been generous with his time and expertise. His insight into fashion gave historical depth and perspective, which greatly enhanced the catalogue and exhibition. In addition, sincere thanks go to Adolfo, Carolina Herrera, Oscar de la Renta, and Valentino, who were all very generous with their contributions. A special thanks is owed to Kenneth Jay Lane for the re-creation of Mrs. Reagan's jewelry. Additionally, we are appreciative of Merv Griffin and Fred Hayman for their enthusiastic support and valuable advice.

We would also like to extend our sincere thanks to the fashion photographer Stefan Studer and his team, Geraldine Baum, Andrei Lucien, Robert Kozek, and Miyuki Fujioka, for capturing the essence and beauty of Mrs. Reagan's dresses. The talented designer of the book, Miko McGinty, and her colleagues Doug Clouse and Rita Jules, as well as the editor Elisa Urbanelli, merit our gratitude for their endless patience and skill in the face of our pressing time constraints.

We would particularly like to thank Jim Warren of Vaudeville Mannequins and Silvestri California for their generous donation of mannequins for the catalogue. Special thanks go to Gerry Clark and David Naranjo of Zing Display for their creation of beautiful mannequins for the exhibition. In addition, I am deeply grateful to the dedicated exhibition design team of WRJ Design Associates for sharing their talents, especially Klaus Baer, Kate Holt, Martis Salma, Cate Andrews, Lily Angotti, Emily Eerdmans, and Riccardo S. Vincenzino, architect, and Manuel Tan of M. K. Tan.

In addition, the following individuals and institutions deserve recognition for their assistance: former White House Chief Usher Gary J. Walters, Administrative Usher Claire A. Faulkner, and Curator Bill Allman; Carrie Street and Sarah Wallerstein of the Prince of Wales Foundation; Harold Koda of the Costume Institute at the Metropolitan Museum of Art; Lee Dunbar of Sotheby's auction house; and Stefanie Prelesnik and Thierry W. Despont.

A very special thanks is extended to Robert M. Higdon, Jr., and Catherine G. Busch for their enormous generosity of time, unending support, and confidence in our endeavor to create a tribute to Mrs. Reagan. Their enthusiasm, knowledge, and guidance throughout the project have been greatly appreciated.

Finally, our most heartfelt thanks go to Mrs. Reagan, whose fascinating life, style, and legacy inspired this exhibition and catalogue. She was very gracious in providing us access to her personal scrapbooks, photographs, letters, and archives, and our questions and requests were always met with patience and kindness. She is truly a very special first lady.

# BIBLIOGRAPHY

Adolfo. Written interview with WRJ Design Associates. June 2007.

Benson, Harry. *The President & Mrs. Reagan: An American Love Story.* New York: Harry N. Abrams, Inc., 2003.

Cannon, Lou. *Governor Reagan: His Rise to Power.* New York: Charles Scribner's Sons, 1994.

_____. *Ronald Reagan: The Presidential Portfolio.* New York: Public Affairs, 2001.

_____. *Ronald Reagan: The Role of a Lifetime.* New York: Public Affairs, 1991; revised edition, 2000.

Colacello, Bob. *Ronnie & Nancy: Their Path to the White House—1911 to 1980.* New York: Warner Books, 2004.

Deaver, Michael K. *A Different Drummer: My Thirty Years with Ronald Reagan.* New York: Harper Collins, 2001.

_____. *Nancy: A Portrait of My Years with Nancy Reagan.* New York: William Morrow, 2004.

de la Renta, Oscar. Written interview with WRJ Design Associates. June 2007.

Galanos, James. Interview with WRJ Design Associates. 2 June 2007.

Hannaford, Peter. *Ronald Reagan and His Ranch: The Western White House, 1981–1989.* Vermont: Images from the Past, 2002.

Hannford, Peter, and Charles D. Hobbs. *Remembering Reagan.* Washington, D.C.: Regnery Publishing, Inc., 1999.

Herrera, Carolina. Written interview with WRJ Design Associates. June 2007.

Hyde, Nina. "Having Designs on the First Lady." *Washington Post,* 18 January 1981.

Kotur, Alexandra. *Carolina Herrera.* New York: Assouline Publishing, Inc., 2004.

Martin, J. J. "Valentino." *Harper's Bazaar* (June 2007).

Noonan, Peggy. *When Character Was King: A Story of Ronald Reagan.* New York: Viking, 2001.

McQuiston, John T. "Mrs. Reagan Pays a Call on Children in Hospital." *New York Times,* 20 December 1983.

Nancy Reagan's personal scrapbooks from the White House. The Ronald Reagan Presidential Library. Simi Valley, California.

The Office of the First Lady's Press Secretary. Press releases. January 1981–January 1989. The Ronald Reagan Presidential Library. Simi Valley, California.

Office of the President-Elect. "Memorandum To: The Cabinet and Executive Officers. Subject: Protocol." Washington, D.C., 19 January 1981.

The Public Papers of the President: Ronald Reagan, 1981–1989. Washington, D.C.: Office of the Federal Register, National Archives and Records Administration; distributed by the United States Government Printing Office.

Radcliffe, Donnie. "Nancy with the Flamenco Feet: Queen Sofia Takes Charge of the First Lady's Outing in Madrid." *Washington Post*, 7 May 1985.

Reagan, Nancy. *I Love You, Ronnie: The Letters of Ronald Reagan to Nancy Reagan.* New York: Random House, 2000; second edition, 2002.

_____. Speeches: The Office of the First Lady. The Ronald Reagan Presidential Library. Simi Valley, California.

Reagan, Nancy, with William Novak. *My Turn: The Memoirs of Nancy Reagan.* New York: Random House, 1989.

Reagan, Nancy, and Ronald Reagan. "What We've Learned About America from Our Years in the White House." *TV Guide,* 28 June 1986.

Reagan, Ronald. *An American Life.* New York: Simon and Schuster, 1990.

Richardson, James D. *A Compilation of Messages and Papers from the Presidents.* Washington, D.C.: Bureau of National Literature, 1911.

*Ronald Reagan, An American Hero: His Voice, His Values, His Vision.* New York: Dorling Kindersley, 2001.

Thatcher, Margaret. Eulogy for Ronald Reagan. 11 June 2004. Margaret Thatcher Foundation.

Wallace, Chris. *First Lady: A Portrait of Nancy Reagan.* New York: St. Martin's Press, 1986.

Zinko, Carolyn. "A New Expression: Fashion Designer James Galanos Finds Salvation—for Now—in Creating Art." *SF Gate* [website of the *San Francisco Chronicle*], 17 September 2006.

*I just want to start each day by opening my eyes and seeing you
and end each day seeing you before I close them. In between times,
I'll just look in my heart. You are always there.*

— RONALD REAGAN

At their Santa Barbara ranch, the president and first lady share a loving moment
overlooking Lake Lucky on their thirtieth wedding anniversary.